More Than a Label

Why What You Wear or Who You're With Doesn't Define Who You Are

Aisha Muharrar

Edited by Elizabeth Verdick

free spirit
PUBLiSHiNG®

Works
for kids®

JACKSON COUNTY LIBRARY SERVICES
MEDFORD OREGON 97501

Library of Congress Cataloging-in-Publication Data
Muharrar, Aisha.
      More than a label : why what you wear and who you're with doesn't define who you are / Aisha Muharrar.
      p. cm.
      Includes bibliographical references and index.
Summary: Drawn from a survey of more than one thousand teenagers, first-person stories help to address the problems inherent in labeling people.
      ISBN 1-57542-110-0 (alk. paper)
      1. Teenagers—Social conditions—Juvenile literature. 2. Adolescent psychology—Juvenile literature. [1. Stereotype (Psychology) 2. Conduct of life.] I. Title.

      HQ796 .M8328 2002
      305.235—dc21   2001007386

At the time of this book's publication, all facts and figures cited are the most current available; all telephone numbers, addresses, and Web site URLs are accurate and active; all publications, organizations, Web sites, and other resources exist as described in this book; and all have been verified. The author and Free Spirit Publishing make no warranty or guarantee concerning the information and materials given out by organizations or content found at Web sites, and we are not responsible for any changes that occur after this book's publication. If you find an error or believe that a resource listed here is not as described, please contact Free Spirit Publishing. Parents, teachers, and other adults: We strongly urge you to monitor children's use of the Internet.

Cover by Percolator
Interior book design by Crysten Puszczykowski
Assistant Editor: Jennifer Brannen
Index compiled by Kay K. Schlembach

10 9 8 7 6 5 4 3 2 1
Printed in the United States of America

Free Spirit Publishing Inc.
217 Fifth Avenue North, Suite 200
Minneapolis, MN 55401-1299
(612) 338-2068
help4kids@freespirit.com
www.freespirit.com

The following are registered trademarks of Free Spirit Publishing Inc.:
FREE SPIRIT®
FREE SPIRIT PUBLISHING®
SELF-HELP FOR TEENS®
SELF-HELP FOR KIDS®
WORKS FOR KIDS®
THE FREE SPIRITED CLASSROOM®

free spirit
PUBLISHING®
Works for kids®

Dedication

To Mom, a superstar in her own right.

Acknowledgments

Many, many special thanks to the teens who wrote essays and filled out the Teen Labels Surveys. Thanks to Judy Galbraith for seeing the importance of a book on this subject. Thanks to my editors, Elizabeth Verdick and Krissy McCurry, and all of the dedicated people at Free Spirit. Thanks to my photographer and friend, Sean "We are not on Udall Road" Collins. And thank you always to my family and friends who supported me through writing this book, high school, and the past 18 years.

Contents

To: Readers
From: Aisha
Subject: More Than a Label

Okay, first things first. You may be wondering how a Long Island teen like myself ends up writing a book about labels. Like so many high school experiences, it can all be traced back to freshman year (for me, that was 1998–99). While drifting off to sleep one night, I began to think about all the different groups of teens in my high school. I had thought about the social groups at my school and other high schools around the nation before. It's hard not to notice that even though labels may not always be said aloud, they're floating around in the high school atmosphere.

That night was different, though. It had only been a few months since the Columbine High School shootings. I was fourteen, and the idea of teens murdering their peers appalled me. I'm sure many other teens were thinking about that tragedy late at night, too.

After Columbine, it was difficult not to think about labels and social groups. The media kept talking about how labels, cliques, bullying, and the pressure to fit in were taking a toll on high school students everywhere. I couldn't help but think that if violence happened at Columbine and other schools, it could happen at any high school. When I later met and talked to two students from Littleton, Colorado (where Columbine High School is), it became even clearer to me that they were just like teens everywhere in America.

I decided to start an anti-violence committee at my high school in tenth grade. I wanted to help maintain the relatively peaceful environment in my school and

1

educate others about how violence erupts. While working on this committee, I corresponded with a national anti-violence/pro-tolerance organization known as SHiNE (read more about SHiNE on page 128). I was the volunteer youth reporter for one of their charity benefits—a really cool concert held by New York radio station Z100, featuring performances by Jennifer Lopez and Smashmouth.

So, I was already interested in preventing violence and promoting respect before I wrote this book. I kept thinking about labels and their role in high school life. I never believed that labels were the sole reason for Columbine—not for a second. But I did understand that labels played a part. I wanted to do something. And I knew that writing was the key.

The summer before my junior year started with a bang. I was selected to be a member of *Teen People*'s News Team. For those of you who may not know, *Teen People* is the youth version of *People* magazine. Each year, *Teen People* announces the search for teens to write articles for the magazine. I applied twice. When I was thirteen, I was rejected; but the second time, I had to send a brief description of myself and a writing sample, and I submitted the article I'd written for SHiNE. I was thrilled when *Teen People* picked me.

As a News Team correspondent, I got to go to the magazine's offices and meet the other teen writers. It was great to get to know such unique and interesting teens from all parts of the country and Canada. Plus, I was published a few times. Maybe you saw my work?

In school, I was still doing what most teens do, hanging out and studying. And I was still thinking about labels. Every time I saw someone get snubbed or teased, I thought more about labels, cliques, and other social dividers at my school. I was friends with a variety of teens who had a variety of labels: one was called a goth, some were called preps and others nerds, some were called freaks. I tended to ignore the social labels and talk to people I liked. But I didn't think it was right that there were all these groups in the first place.

The labels didn't matter much to me, but I noticed they mattered to others. My friends in one group often would make fun of my friends in another. No matter how popular or unpopular the group was, there was some other group it didn't want to associate with or tried to avoid. Why didn't they like each other? Some didn't even know each other—they based their opinions solely on labels. I understood, though, that labels never gave the full picture. I couldn't have described each friend with just one label—so how could other people do it so easily?

I was frustrated by the unspoken rules that seemed to govern high school life. To me, the labels that people gave each other—or themselves—were like invisible name tags. Once you started to "wear" one, everyone was free to make assumptions about who you are.

I began to ask myself questions about teens and labeling. Who actually hands out these labels? What role do the labels play? Do they help or harm? Do people like their labels? Do they hate them? Are they even aware of them? What's the truth behind all these labels? That's what I wanted to find out—and that's how this book began.

Ever since I was a kid, I've loved books and wanted to write one of my own. I put together a book proposal and sent it to a publisher who specializes in books that help teens. As it turns out, the publisher was interested in the labeling phenomenon, too. How do teens across America feel about labeling? What are the positive and negative effects? Together, we were about to find out.

We developed the Teen Labels Survey (see the survey on pages 7–9) and sent it out to teens ages thirteen to eighteen in all regions of the country. Over one thousand teens from urban or rural areas, suburbs, and small towns responded. Their perspectives, opinions, and experiences helped shape this book. I'd like to thank each and every one of them for helping me out!

That's how *More Than a Label* got its start. I hope you enjoy this book. If you want to tell me what you think of it or how labeling has affected you, you can write to me in care of:

Free Spirit Publishing Inc.
217 Fifth Avenue North, Suite 200
Minneapolis, MN 55401-1299

Email: help4kids@freespirit.com

I look forward to hearing from you!

Aisha Muharrar

ABOUT THIS BOOK

Time for a lesson in book navigation. This is your book, so I'm not going to tell you what you should read first or how you should read it: front to back, back to front, whatever way you want. I will tell you how it's organized, though:

- Part 1, "What's in a Label?" explains what labels are and how they develop.
- Part 2, "How Labels Make People Feel," is about the many emotions—positive and negative—that go along with labels.
- Part 3, "What You Can Do About Labeling," includes ideas for breaking the labeling habit and ways you can help yourself and others.

Every chapter of the book contains quotes from the Teen Labels Survey, so you can find out what other teens think and how they feel. You'll also get to read personal essays written by teens about labels, cliques, and the social pressures they've faced. I've included activities you can try, and lots of resources if you're interested in learning more about any of the topics I've written about.

As you'll see, this book is filled with many voices. I wanted to share the different ideas, thoughts, opinions, feelings, and experiences of teens of all ages and backgrounds. Some of these teens may be like you, and some may not. Some of them label, some don't. Some are in cliques, while others avoid them. I included a variety of perspectives because labels mean different things to different people. You get to make up your own mind about what they mean to you.

By now, you may be wondering what I think about labels. Before doing the survey, I was convinced that labels are damaging, both socially and emotionally. I've seen my own friends label each other and let rumors or gossip influence their opinions of others. I myself have let stereotypes get in the way of making friends with people. I thought labels were totally negative . . . but then I found out that plenty of teens *like* their labels and feel proud of them. I began to think more deeply about what labels are all about.

As you'll find out, labels can be both bad *and* good. But there's one thing I know for sure: *You are more than a label.* I think every teen has the right to be viewed as an individual. And all of us need to be able to look beyond labels to find out who we really are.

I certainly don't expect to solve the social problems in American high schools by writing this book. But I do hope reading *More Than a Label* will do three simple things for you:

#1 Show you the importance of looking beyond labels. Just because you're labeled as this, and someone else is labeled as that, doesn't mean you have nothing in common. You may discover that you're more alike than you thought. Okay, so you're not going to skip off together into a field of daisies; but you might decide to get to know someone you never thought you'd want to know.

#2 Give you a glimpse into how other teens feel. Reading the quotes and essays by teens will let you step into their shoes and see life from other points of view. This may give you a new perspective or even change your opinion of people you've labeled in the past.

#3 Let you be yourself. Other people don't define you. *You* define you. It's okay to have interests and goals that are different from the majority of people you know. It's okay to stand out. It's okay to have friends from different groups. And it's okay to be yourself, instead of trying to fit a label. You have every right to identify yourself as you wish, and to put that "Everyone thinks I'm . . . " feeling behind you.

I once saw a poster that said:

LABELS ARE FOR JARS.

I couldn't agree more.

The Teen Labels Survey

A. Demographics

Your age: _____

Your gender: (circle one)   Male   Female

Where you live: (circle one)
Urban Area   Suburb   Small Town   Rural Area
Other:_____

B. Labels (Preppy/Prep, Goth, Nerd/Geek, Thug, Jock, Slut, Scrub, Freak, Raverz, Skater, Punk, Surferchick/Surferdude, Loner, Drama Kid, Alties, Chicas, Hippie, Homie-G, Goody-Goody, Floater, Stoner, Wannabe, Teen Queen, Techie, Straight-Edge . . .)

B1: Have you ever been labeled? (circle one)   Yes   No

B2: Which of the above labels, if any, have you been called or associated with? Please list:

B3: Were you called any label not listed above, and if so, what was it?

B4: How did you feel about the label(s) you were given? Please explain:

B5: Describe why you think you may have been labeled in these ways. For example, do the labels seem to be connected to your appearance? To your racial or ethnic background? To your family's financial background? To a stereotype? To your level of popularity? Please explain:

B6: Do you think girls are labeled more often than guys, or vice versa? Or do you think that labels affect girls and guys equally? Please explain:

B7: Do you label your peers? Why or why not?

B8: Do you label yourself? (circle one)   Yes   No
If yes, see question #B9 below. If no, please explain:

B9: If you do use a label to describe yourself, how does the label make you feel about who you are? Please explain:

C. Cliques & Popularity

C1: Does your school have cliques? (circle one)   Yes   No

C2: How do you define or describe a clique?

C3: Do you consider you and your friends a clique?
Why or why not?

C4: If your school has cliques, what do you think draws them together?

C5: Do you think labels, popularity, and cliques are related? Why or why not?

C6: Which label is most associated with popularity in your high school?_____
Which label is least associated with popularity?

_____

C7: Do you feel like you "fit in" at school? Why or why not?

C8: If you could change one thing about the social scene at your school, what would it be?

C9: How does your social life at school affect other aspects of your life and how you see yourself?

Part 1
WHAT'S IN A LABEL?

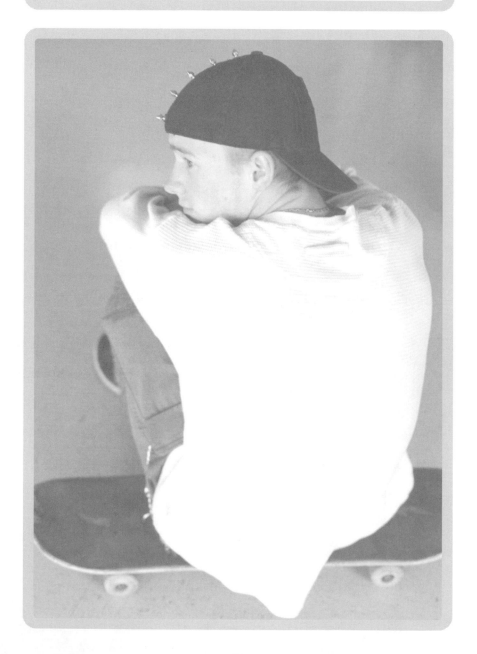

CHAPTER 1

Why Is Labeling Such a Big Deal?

"Labels are like the back of a book, a brief summary."
From the Teen Labels Survey

It's four minutes before first period at your typical high school. Lockers are slamming as everyone scrambles to get to class. So many voices are mingled together that you can't even hear what anyone's saying. Listen closer:

"This hallway's closed—to geeks."

"She's hot, but my boys would never let me live down dating some skank."

"Looks like somebody just fell out of a J.Crew catalog. Preps are such clones."

"He's a thug!"

Labels. They're everywhere. You hear them at school and out in the world. They're a part of our language. Labels are so fixed in everyday speech that you may not even think twice about them.

What exactly *is* a label? Here's my own definition:

LABEL:

A word used to define or make assumptions about an individual. Labels are usually based on how someone looks, dresses, acts, or talks—or who the person hangs out with.

Labels are simple words, but they have a powerful impact. Every time you use one, you're narrowing your impression of

11

someone else. You're letting one word describe someone as a "type." That person is no longer seen as an individual because the label says it all.

We often use labels automatically, and each time we do we recall (on some level):

• where we've heard the label before

• what our friends think about it

• how it's used socially

• the characteristics usually associated with the label

On the surface, labels seem to simplify the process of getting to know other people. You don't even have to meet the person who's being labeled—the label you've heard is the only introduction you need . . . or is it?

Suppose your friends are talking about a girl from some other school. You don't know her, but you hear she is the captain of both the girls' soccer and lacrosse teams, has a strong, muscular body, and spends most of her free time with members of her sports teams. What label might you and your friends give her? The answer's easy: jock.

You didn't come to that conclusion all by yourself—you had help from society. It's common knowledge that jock = athlete. But this equation isn't quite so simple. When you think about it, different people have different ideas about what the term jock may imply.

For some, jock suggests a person who's overly aggressive on and off the field—maybe even a bully. Others may decide that jocks are more focused on athletics than academics, and therefore aren't very smart. Still others may believe that being a jock means you're in the cool crowd, because sports are so popular at many schools—or that someone who's into sports is a natural leader. Some people may even mistakenly believe that a girl jock is trying to be a "boy," since she's muscular and athletic. (What a joke!)

Do any of these assumptions about the jock label sound familiar? Jock is one label found in almost every school. If you haven't heard it at your own school, you've probably seen TV shows or movies that portray teen athletes as either popular and admired, or as beer-guzzling jerks who pick on people smaller than they are.

Going back to the girl from another school, the one you haven't met but who's labeled a jock: Based on your assumptions about jocks, do you think she's someone worth knowing or someone you'll avoid? Unless you're 100 percent "label proof" (and I'm not sure anyone actually is), you might make a decision before you've got all the facts. This is labeling in action.

Some labels—like jock—are almost universal. Others aren't as familiar. Your school probably has well-known and not-so-well-known labels, just like other schools throughout the country. On the next page are the labels that many teens wrote about on the Teen Labels Survey.

The Labels List*

`ABERCROMBIE:` another name for a prep (see next page)

`ALTIE:` nonconformist, likes alternative music

`CHEERLEADER:` athletic, shallow, P-E-R-K-Y

`DITZ:` like a teen queen (see next page), really dopey

`DRAMA KID:` performer, diva attitude, "deep"

`FLOATER:` "in and out," fits anywhere

`FREAK:` not ordinary, multiple piercings, dyed hair

`GAMER:` like a player (see next page) or into video games

`GANGSTA:` influenced by gangsta rap, troublemaker, criminal

`GEEK:` expert in something, loves to learn, ignores popular trends, possibly dorky

`GOODY-GOODY:` honor student, volunteer, teacher's favorite

`GOTH:` black clothing, black makeup, quiet and pensive

`HIP-HOPPER:` likes hip-hop music, baggy clothes

`HIPPIE:` '60s look, free spirit, protest buttons

`HOMIE-G:` tough, likes rap, wears baggy clothes

`INDIE:` bohemian clothes, *au natural,* most likely to be voted unique

`JOCK:` strong, athletic, could be dumb

*The fine print: I knew I'd have to put in a disclaimer when I made this labels list. Keep in mind that I've defined the labels based on what I know personally and what I've heard from teens I've talked to or surveyed. The way I describe a certain label here may not be the way you describe it, but please don't get upset with me and send letters like "I'm a homie-g and I hate baggy clothes. You are so wrong about me." Labels aren't known for showing the full picture of a person; they're often based on our own experiences and perceptions. If anything, this list shows how crazy the labeling process actually is!

LONER: no clique, few friends

LOSER: the word speaks for itself

NERD: smart, awkward, shy, may be a loser

PLAYER: a.k.a "playa," goes out with more than one person at a time

POSER: fake, like a wannabe (see below)

PREP/PREPPY: short for prep school, "old money," lacrosse games/tennis matches

PUNK: likes punk music, rebellious

RAVER/RAVERZ: goes to rave parties, associated with E (the drug, not Entertainment Television)

SCRUB: unkempt, not worth anyone's time, broke

SKANK: think bare midriff and short skirts, overly flirty, would have sex

SKATER: into punk culture, skateboards, long shorts, and big, bright T-shirts

SLUT: like a "skank," rumored to have slept around, looks like someone who sleeps around

STONER: on drugs, laid back, mellow but totally lazy

STRAIGHT-EDGE: into rock music, but not sex and drugs

SURFERCHICK/SURFERDUDE: likes to surf, tan, and hang out

TECHIE: likes to play with computers, watches *Star Trek* (oops, that's a "Trekkie")

TEEN QUEEN: pop music fan, shopper, trendy, a ditz or teenybopper

THUG: dangerous, a bully

WANNABE: tries too hard to be a certain label, completely fake

TRY IT!

What's one label that's always interested you or interests you now? To find out more about it, look up its original meaning in the dictionary (if you can find its definition), try an Internet search engine, or just ask your friends and family what they know about it.

Labels vs. Slurs and Name-calling

For some reason, when I think about name-calling, elementary school comes to mind. When I think of labels, I think about middle school and high school. But one thing I found out from the surveys is that the lines between labels, name-calling, and slurs are pretty fuzzy. Many teens who responded to the survey said they had been called things like rich kid, fatty, spaz, weirdo, country boy, teacher's pet, outcast, moron, dumb blond, tomboy, prude, snob, or shorty.

In this book, I'm mostly talking about labels, which I think are different from name-calling or any kind of nicknaming (nicknames are usually given with affection or for fun). Take the name shorty, for example. If someone always calls you shorty because you're small for your age, this isn't necessarily a label. When you think about it, shorty doesn't define a *type* of person. On the other hand, most people can come up with a specific image if they hear a label like drama kid. They think of a melodramatic person, maybe even in full Hamlet costume, with a supreme-diva attitude. In other words, a whole set of characteristics often can be associated with that label.

> "I've been called names due to my racial background, which kills me. I remember when I was younger someone said, 'Get out of that seat you chink.' (I'm Filipino.) I said, 'Well, if you're going to make fun of me, at least use the right race. It's 'Get out of that seat you Flip.'"
> —Girl, 17

Sure, a name like shorty could be turned into a label—almost any descriptive term could be if it's used to refer to a specific *type* of person. If the term shorty also came to imply something about someone's intelligence, interests, or activities, then it would be a label. But there probably would never be a shorty *group,* with teens who all hang out together because of their height. In general, labels carry with them a *group* of characteristics that describe a group of people.

> "Often, people would judge me or my handicap and maintain this sort of fear of me. I was called 'deaf' and 'dumb.' Lots of kids didn't try to be my friend, so I had to go out and make my own friends. Sometimes I felt that my handicap made me stick out too much."
> —Girl, 18

If people always call you by a certain name, it can begin to *feel* like a label. For example, if you're called skinny or twig, it may seem as if people only view you that way. They don't see that there's more to you than one aspect of your appearance. Still, the name isn't a label because it doesn't attempt to define a group of characteristics you may have in common with a group of people. (That doesn't mean the name hurts any less, though.)

Slurs are another kind of name-calling, based on only one aspect of someone's appearance or background. When I saw the survey results, I realized that a huge number of teens had been the victims of slurs—or words that attack your race, religion, gender, or sexual orientation.

These words are incredibly offensive to many people, including me. Slurs are generally seen as "bad words"—the kind of stuff you wouldn't be able to say on national television or in polite conversation. (No one's ever heard of bleeping out *scrub* or *geek,* right?) Many teens who filled out the survey had been the victims of horrible slurs such as queer, whore, chink, gook, nigger, dyke, honky, JAP (Jewish American Princess), faggot, Jesus freak, white trash, gimp, or flamer. I know that many people reading this book might be shocked to see these words in print, but I wanted everyone to realize that these words *aren't* labels—they're slurs, and they hurt *way* more than a label ever could. Unfortunately, slurs are a real part of teens' lives and may be almost as common as labels. (See pages 83–85 and 91–107 for more about how slurs are used and how they make people feel.)

Labels Yesterday and Today

86%
of teens said
they had been
labeled!

If your school is anything like other schools across the nation, labels are an unavoidable part of the social makeup. According to the Teen Labels Survey, 86 percent of teens said they had been labeled. If you do the math, this means only 14 percent of teens surveyed hadn't been labeled. Of those 14 percent, some may have had labels they didn't even know about.

When I found out that the majority of teens surveyed had been labeled, I wondered if labels had always been such a big deal or if they were something new. I did a little research into the social history of twentieth-century America and learned some interesting things. Labels not only come and go, they even get recycled and often reinvented by each generation that uses them. Punks, hippies, preppies, and stoners have all outlasted the decades that coined them. And some labels, like nerd, jock, and goody-goody seem almost timeless.

Here are a few highlights of labels through the ages:

1950s
In the "fabulous fifties," some teens were known as greasers (think John Travolta in the movie *Grease*) or squares (think letter jackets and poodle skirts). Babies born during the fifties and sixties have been collectively labeled as Baby Boomers, because the population of babies boomed during those years.

1960s
According to the book *Sixties People* by Jane and Michael Stern, "the sixties was a time when you could tell just by looking at someone where they stood politically, socially, or philosophically." The Sterns say people could be identified as perky girls, surfers, hippies, rebels, playboys, or folkniks (just to name a few).

1970s

Disco ruled with its disco queens and freaks. AM radio transformed into FM, and hard rock dominated the airwaves as metalheads, rockers, and stoners tuned in. Glam rockers experimented with makeup and cross-dressing. For the first time, punks took the cultural stage, reinventing the look of rebellion.

1980s

Teens of the eighties, once dubbed Generation X, were continually portrayed as self-absorbed and lazy. Divided into sub-groups, Gen-Xers also were known as punks, preppies (a preppy handbook was even sold in stores), goths, brains, slackers, freaks, and valley girls (those mall-obsessed teens who spoke quickly with a lot of "likes" in their sentences—like, you know what I, like, mean?). Labels such as straight-edge, skaters, and raverz made their first appearances. The older Gen-Xers (in their twenties) were known as yuppies—short for young urban professionals.

1990s

The Gen-X label continued, and new ones were added: Generation Y and Millennials (a name that refers to anyone born 1982–2000). Technology, globalization, grunge, and hip-hop culture ruled the day. Thugs, homies, and scrubs walked the halls with techies, raverz, and alties. And even geek started to become chic with the rise of dot.com culture.

Today, labels are even more widespread than they were in the past. Why is this? One reason is that familiar old warning: "Kids are growing up too fast these days." Not to sound like a little old lady, but when I saw an eight-year-old dressed in a halter top and low-rise hip huggers, I was kind of shocked. When I was eight, I was happy to wear leggings and turtlenecks. Obviously, fashions change with the times, but have you noticed that young kids today often try to dress like teens or adults? Kids are pressuring each other to be sexually active in *middle* school. This makes me wonder if kids and teens really are growing up too fast.

How is this connected to labels? Kids and preteens are exposed to lots of different images at an early age through TV, movies, videos, magazines, and commercials. Before they're even teens, they may start imitating their favorite celebrities by dressing, talking, or behaving in certain ways. This adds up to pressure to be cool or popular earlier in life. Kids begin looking for ways to define themselves and their peers.

That's where labels come into the picture. Teens often look to define themselves and each other by traits they hold in common. Whatever the label may be, there's most likely a group it belongs to. The labels then carry on into high school and form the basis of each school's social scene.

Because many families today have a single parent or two parents who work, teens tend to spend more and more time with friends. A group of friends may even become a second family, creating a bond that's stronger—and sometimes more influential—than the one at home. To identify with the group (and sometimes that group is a clique or a gang), teens may wear specific clothes or have rules of behavior. Their label becomes a part of their identity and helps to establish their belonging to the group of their choice.

Modern technologies play a role, too. As the first generation to grow up with computers, we can go on the Internet as quickly and easily as our parents dialed a phone. The greatest advantages of living in an age of technology are the communication possibilities. With a point and click, we can connect with our best friend or with teens around the world. The Internet hosts chats and Web sites for nearly every interest on the planet, letting teens express themselves freely and feel a sense of belonging. As a result, the Internet helps create labels and spread their use. Even regional labels can quickly become national slang with the help of chat rooms and other online communication.

So, what's my point? Labels have worked their way into our culture and our everyday lives. But I see them as a cop out. You don't have to get to know someone if his or her label, in your mind, already speaks volumes. You end up excluding whole groups of people from your list of who matters if you decide not to associate with certain types. Or *they* can end up excluding *you* because of their opinions based on your label.

I know there are teens who say they love and are proud of their labels, and if you're one of them, my goal isn't to convince you that you're wrong. I just want you, and anyone else reading this book, to consider the fact that a person is so much more than a label. Even if you like your label because you like some of the things it may represent, you're letting in the bad with the good.

Once you're identified with a label, people can use it to make all kinds of judgments about you. You may have many of the characteristics associated with your label, but you probably don't have *all* of them! If every person who had the same label had all of the supposed characteristics of that label, they would all be the same person. Because that's impossible, it's impossible for a label to give you a clear picture of an individual—there's *always* more to a person than a label allows you to see.

I WAS LABELED, TOO...

Ever since the first grade, I've been haunted by a label that may not seem like a bad thing to my classmates, but it has put me in the middle of many debates with them about who I really am. My closest friends and I have always been called goody-goodies, even though we never were teachers' pets. People who were our friends talked about us behind our backs, and whether they realized it or not, they hurt us at times. All we ever did to deserve this label was make good grades in gifted classes. I have always felt that the labeling stemmed from jealousy and misunderstanding.

Now, I can't say this label has held me back in any way. I have lots of friends from all walks of life, I'm in and have been president of several school clubs, I play sports, and I generally can get along with anybody.

However, I feel very lucky because I seem to be an exception to the effects of this label. Some of my friends haven't always been as fortunate and still have trouble shaking their reputations. Even I sometimes wish that certain people would step back and get to know me for who I really am, instead of taking me for who they think I am. It bothers me that everyone I meet in school already has a preconceived idea about what I'm like.

I feel as if I want to stand up and tell those people everything I really am: a writer, a music lover, an athlete, and a person who loves animals, beaches, dancing, singing, reading, and laughing until it hurts. Maybe then they would understand me a little better.

While I don't agree with labels, especially when they're used to taunt and tease, I can see how they might develop. What we all need to learn to do is keep those notions to ourselves and be open-minded when we meet new people. As goody-goody as that may sound, that's completely how I feel. But of course, it only says a little about who I am.—*Amanda H.*

. . . AND I'M MORE THAN A LABEL

When Asked...

Do you label your peers? Why or why not?

Teens Answered...

(The Yes's)

"If anyone answers no to this question, they're lying."
—*Girl, 16*

"I think that we are almost forced, for public identification/social purposes to label."—*Girl, 15*

"Yes, of course. I don't believe a single person who denies that they do. I use two main labels: like me or not like me."—*Guy, 15*

"I do sometimes label my peers, not necessarily because I'm being mean but sometimes it's just easier to describe people that way."—*Girl, 16*

"Yes, I judge everyone around me who's at school."
—*Guy, 16*

"Yes, because now labels kind of just come along with life and it seems like a natural thing to do."—*Girl, 16*

"Yeah, because some of us are geeks, jocks, and skaters. If we didn't have these labels, we'd all be the same and that would be boring."—*Guy, 14*

"Yes, it's an easy way to identify people."—*Girl, 16*

"Yes, because they labeled me."—*Guy, 16*

"Yes, unfortunately . . . I think it's a natural thing that everyone does because we are scared to dig deeper and find out more about a person who is different than we are. People are scared of what they don't know."—*Girl, 17*

"Yes, it's so common. Everyone runs on snap judgments and first impressions."—*Girl, 15*

"Mentally I may label people, but I never call them by those names."—*Guy, 17*

"I label my peers, it's kind of like a game."—*Girl, 16*

"Doesn't everyone?"—*Guy, 15*

(The Nos)

"No, I know how it hurt me and I don't see the point to doing it to anyone else."—*Girl, 15*

"No, each person deserves to be treated as an individual, not as a stereotype."—*Girl, 16*

"Not usually. It's just not cool to do that."—*Guy, 16*

"No, because it's up to them how they want to be." —*Girl, 14*

"No! Because why should I?!"—*Guy, 13*

"I try not to. What's the point? It's just mean and shows *your* confidence issues."—*Girl, 17*

"No, I don't prejudge anyone before I get to know them. I treat everyone with respect."—*Guy, 16*

"No. *Judge not lest ye be judged.* Just kidding. I do think labeling is wrong and useless."—*Girl, 17*

"I wouldn't want them to label me. So I'm not going to label them."—*Girl, 15*

"No. Labeling my peers is prejudice, and prejudice is ignorance."—*Guy, 17*

"No, because I would not want to stoop so low."—*Girl, 14*

So, Is There a "Right" Answer?

Wouldn't it be easier if there was? The teens who responded to the survey obviously had their reasons for labeling or not labeling. It's interesting that some teens who said *yes* to labeling pointed out that labeling makes things simpler. As human beings, we like to put things into categories so they're easier to understand and communicate about. We categorize our to-do lists. We categorize different types of food at the grocery store. We categorize our clothes by style, season, and clean or dirty. For some reason, we feel the need to categorize people as well. It's sociology 101.

Does labeling *actually* simplify—or does it make life more complicated? In some ways, it does both. That's what makes labeling so confusing.

CHAPTER 2

How Labels Develop

"Why do we have to be called nerds just because we get straight A's? Why do we get called jocks when we play a sport? What is the point of judging people on what they do and like? Wouldn't everything be easier if we didn't have labels? So why do we?"
From the Teen Labels Survey

Where do labels come from? How do we know which label to assign to someone else? Why are certain looks and behaviors only associated with certain labels? How can we know if frozen fish sticks are stale? I'm kidding about that one—but the first three questions are serious.

Partly, we label to try to make life simpler. We skip the part about getting to know someone and go straight to making assumptions. This saves us the trouble of connecting an individual identity with every individual. It actually sounds silly—we don't have enough time to get to know someone?

Teens who filled out the Teen Labels Survey offered different opinions about why we label each other and what these labels are based on. This information helped me put together a list of five factors most commonly associated with labeling. Before I tell you what those factors are . . .

TRY IT!

The factors most commonly associated with labeling are ones that all people share. What would you guess they are? Grab a piece of paper and write them down; if you'd like, also write why you think each one contributes to labeling.

The Five Factors

We look at these factors and make a decision about what label to give to others.

1. Clothing Style/Appearance

2. Interests/Activities/Music Preferences

3. Behavior/Personality

4. Grades/Intellect

5. Friends

These are the social factors mentioned by most teens, but other factors came up, too, including: *wealth* (or lack of it), *race or ethnic background, religion, hometown,* and being *male or female.* With the possible exception of religion, these aren't things teens can choose about themselves or their families. The five factors below are about less absolute traits.

#1 Clothing Style/Appearance

A group of sophomore girls is gathered near their lockers, and it's a wonder they're not human popsicles because it's only 50 degrees outside and they're wearing tube tops and mini skirts. They flirtatiously smile as a senior guy passes by. Nearby, a bunch of freshman guys are swapping CDs, stuffing the cases in the pockets of their oversized puffy jackets and baggy jeans. Another group of friends, wearing khakis and pastel T-shirts, is laughing about what happened at a party over the weekend. On any given morning, this could be the scene at my high school—or yours. You can probably figure out each group's label from their clothing.

According to the teens who were surveyed, labels based on how you dress depend on:

• the logo or brand name on your clothes

• the kind of people who dress the same way at your school

- how celebrities wear these styles or how the media portrays the clothes

- how much or how little clothing you wear

Labels on clothes seem to make a big difference when it comes to labels on *people*. When you think about specific stores and designers, can't you just picture someone who would wear their clothes? If you've seen their ads in magazines or on TV, you know what the target market is—which means you know what a teen who wears a certain brand or logo is "supposed" to look like.

One label that's given to a lot of teens, Abercrombie, actually takes its name from a clothing store. The label is supposed to be a synonym for prep because the store sells preppy-style clothes. Does this mean that there's a sign outside the store that states: "Do not enter unless you're a prep"? Not that I've ever seen.

In the 1940s, the term *Abercrombie* meant "know-it-all."

Some groups of friends always shop at the same stores and tend to dress alike. Other groups may choose clothes that go against the norm (for example, goths who wear all black or hippies who wear tie-dyed shirts and protest buttons). In this way, specific styles almost become uniforms for specific labels.

Sometimes teens dress like their favorite celebrities as a way to show that they're fans of someone or to get attention (since celebrities get loads of attention in our society). Back in the 1980s, Madonna had girls around the country so in love with her style that they began to imitate every aspect of her wardrobe. They became known as

"How can the fact that I wear Abercrombie mean I'm a ditzy prep? It can't! And that's what upsets me."
—Girl, 15

Madonna Wannabes. Does this sound a little like a pop-star phenomenon of our generation? Yep, "Little Britneys," as they're known, copy the fashions of singer Britney Spears. Rappers like P. Diddy and Nelly have guys across the country wearing hot sports jerseys, baggy pants, and stocking caps. If you incorporate a "celeb's" style into your wardrobe, people may associate you with that famous person and label you accordingly.

This isn't anything new—teens have been copying the styles of their favorite music, TV, and movie stars for generations. I have to admit I've had my own moments of celebrity influence and peer pleasing. When I was in middle school, I realized that I had the same sneakers as the character Lucy from the TV show *7th Heaven.*

> "A girl could wear a T-shirt and be called a 'ho,' but guys who show their nasty boxers coming out of the tops of their pants aren't called anything."—Girl, 16

My mom got the shoes for me, and before I noticed that they were on television, I didn't really like them. When I saw Lucy wearing them, I was suddenly very proud of my sneakers. They were cool; they were hip. No one else had them, except for a girl on television. I am really embarrassed to be telling this story, let alone what I'm about to say next, but I would actually tell people my sneakers were on *7th Heaven.* They'd say, "Nice shoes." I'd say, "Thanks. You know the girl from *7th Heaven* wears them on the show?" Isn't it odd how my opinion of good taste changed because of a television character? They were still the same shoes, but suddenly I saw them as cool because a celebrity wore them.

Another aspect to consider is how *much* clothing you wear. How long are your shorts or skirts, how tight are your clothes, and how much material is between someone's eyes and your flesh? When you wear clothes that show off your body, people tend to assume that you're okay with engaging in sexual activities, whether it's true or not. This may lead to a label like slut or skank (variations include whore, "ho," or tease). Sometimes girls get these labels from wearing a short skirt or showing some cleavage. It can depend on whether most girls in a school dress this way. If they do, these clothes may be seen as okay to wear; but a girl who stands out for wearing skimpy clothes or tight tops and pants may be labeled for it. Girls tend to get these labels more often than guys, but guys can be called sluts, too. (To read more about the differences between male/female labels, see Chapter 5, "Guy vs. Girl Labeling," on pages 80–90.)

There's definitely a double standard at work here. Sexy clothes for guys usually aren't made to reveal as much skin as those made for girls. Have you ever seen halter tops and micro-mini skirts for guys? If you're a guy, you really have to make an effort to show off your body when you dress. The one exception may be muscle shirts (also known as "wife-beaters"—don't even get me started on this term!). Guys who wear muscle shirts usually have large muscles and may get labeled players or jocks because of how they look and dress.

What you wear can be an influence, but so can how you *look*—your hairstyle, piercings, makeup, and complexion. For example, people of African-American heritage are most likely to be associated with the hip-hopper label because most hip-hop artists are African American. The assumption is that your skin color is a clue to

"I'm labeled a goth because I usually dress in all black. I'm pretty depressed so I don't seem too enthusiastic, I'm quiet, I'm unpopular, and I'm glad that I am. Also, I have a pretty pale complexion."—Guy, 15

what type of music you listen to and what type of life you lead. On the other hand, if your skin is very pale you might be labeled a goth. This is because gothic culture is linked to vampires, and vampires are pale. Here's a label that's *definitely* based on a legend.

When people don't have smooth, clear skin, they might be labeled nerds or even scrubs. This is because our culture values things that appear "perfect" or "flawless," and that standard applies to our faces. The assumption is that if you have a skin problem, it's because you don't care enough about your appearance to put in the time to make it perfect. Does anyone *really* believe that? Yet, the label is there.

The amount of makeup you wear or don't wear can play a surprisingly significant role in being labeled. If you're a boy who wears makeup, you might be labeled a goth, a freak, or a wannabe girl. If you're a girl who wears a lot of makeup, you could be labeled a slut. If you're a girl who doesn't wear makeup, you might be called a prude, a goody-goody, an indie, or a hippie.

Like makeup, piercing is a small thing that can be a big deal. Teens who have multiple piercings (besides earrings) are sometimes labeled freaks. Often, it's assumed that the decision to pierce also makes a statement about someone's values, interests, and attitude. But the piercing is just a hole—not necessarily a way of life.

Hairstyles can lead to labels, too. Take a moment to think about the number of movies or TV shows that have used the old cliché of the girl (sometimes the guy) with shaggy, dirty, or unstyled hair—apparently, the sign of a geek or a nerd. Then, presto, a total hair metamorphosis takes place and the former geek is suddenly cool.

Is hair ever *that* symbolic and life changing? A hairstyle—like any other feature of your appearance—can make a statement about you, but it's not who you are as a person.

TRY IT!

Okay, this is just for fun. If you've watched any television in the past ten years, or opened your eyes even once at school, I bet you can match these hairstyles to the label they're commonly connected with.

1. mohawk	a. surfer
2. long, flowing locks	b. punk
3. crew cut	c. raver
4. dyed hair	d. prep
5. bleached blond	e. hippie

Answers: 1(b), 2(e), 3(d), 4(c), 5(a)

#2 Interests/Activities/Music Preferences

Like most people, you probably build friendships with those who have the same interests as you do (sports, band, clubs, drama, volunteering, academics). Why do certain labels—and the characteristics associated with them—get connected with certain activities? We don't need to go into a scientific study. We can find out for ourselves by considering what we already know about some common interests among high school students.

Take sports and the jock label, for example. Jocks are associated with sports, which are aggressive activities. When I was on my school's soccer team, the phrase I heard most was, "Be aggressive!" Being aggressive leads to winning. If the other team has the ball, you have to get it. If you're supposed to kick the ball, you don't lightly tap it—you draw your leg back and boot the ball with all your strength. Athletes who play hard may appear to be aggressive and tough, and perhaps even hyper because their adrenaline is high during games. Bullies tend to be aggressive, tough, and hyper—maybe this is why jocks are sometimes seen as bullies.

> "I think my indie label came from the music I like and the friends I hang around. My geek/nerd label is because I started a group, the 'Fellowship of Collectors Card Game Players,' and because I'm an integral member of the Chess Club."—Guy, 16

Some sports are even portrayed as barbaric. Barbarians aren't exactly known for their mental aptitude, which could help explain the "dumb jock" label. Another explanation? The idea (sometimes based on fact) that athletes may focus on sports to the exclusion of academics. Their grades may slide, but as long as they're performing well on the court or field, they get by. The truth is, many athletes work just as hard in class as anybody else. Plus, it takes a lot of concentration to remember the complicated rules and strategies of sports. Whether you play a sport or not isn't a measure of your intelligence.

As with sports, certain clubs or extracurricular activities can lead to friendships—and labels. For example, if you're interested in theater and you get involved in your school's drama club, you're likely to find other people who love *My Fair Lady* as much as you do and who actually know that "stage right" means the left side when you're sitting in the audience. Spending all of that time together rehearsing lines and building sets usually leads to friendships. That huge time commitment also lends itself to the idea of the obsessed drama kid who only cares about plays and musicals. Sure, it takes a lot of work and time to put on a school production, but this doesn't mean everyone involved *lives for* drama. For some reason, people who are into the drama scene might be labeled as drama queens (meaning they overact and overreact).

> "I like my geek label. My geekiness is probably where my job is coming from someday."—Guy, 15

Today, an interest in computers and technology is common among a lot of teens. If you're into these things, you'll eventually figure out which of your classmates you can call to discuss RAM and MP3s. Soon talking about your favorite solutions to technological glitches could lead to hanging out together. Two of my friends, who have bonded over computers since the fourth grade, even started a Web business together.

The rise in computer know-how has given rise to new labels like computer geek and techie. Why are teens who have a real understanding of computers labeled like this? Computers have special acronyms for complicated programs, can perform functions faster than a human can, and take some technical expertise to understand—in other words, computers may seem like complicated beasts to tame. Many people are capable of word processing or surfing the Internet, but fewer understand the deeper complexities of the computer world. So when a teen knows more about computer technology than many adults, it's assumed that the teen has great intellectual ability—a trait that may or may not be admired. The assumption then gets taken a step further: intellectual ability = social *in*ability.

How did that assumption develop? Computer aptitude suggests that you spend a lot of time learning about computers—and that's a lot of time spent indoors in front of a machine. This has led to a stereotype of someone who's pale and unathletic—someone who needs glasses because of long hours spent staring at a screen. People presume that a person fitting this description is also antisocial, and perhaps only has friends through the Internet, instead of through live social interaction. Thus, the stereotype—and label—of computer geeks and techies was born.

I WAS LABELED, TOO...

The dictionary defines geek as: "*Slang.* Any strange or eccentric person." However, this is not the definition of geek that we have come to know. Nowadays, geeks are more commonly accepted as smart people with thick glasses and exceptional computer skills. I have looked and looked for this type of person, but I can't find one anywhere. So here is the *modified* definition of geek that I offer: "Any slightly odd or weird person who excels best when working with a computer."

Geeks are widely known for their larger-than-life attitude and sometimes for big egos. I know this for a fact because I too suffer from an overworked ego. Yes, I am a geek. The always-handy calculator and pencil behind the ear are sure signs of my geekiness. The first thing that a non-geek is likely to notice about me is my intelligence. Imagine this: it's the first day of class and I walk in, pencil behind my ear, calculator in hand. Everyone is going to stare because there is a certain aura that says, "I belong here. I like to learn, I want to learn, and I love my computer."

You can tell a geek from his or her appearance. Boy geeks, though extremely bright, don't care much about their appearance; slacks or jeans and a long-sleeved shirt usually satisfy their needs. The girl geeks, however, may try to dress "in." It never succeeds because we're too busy working on our computers to pay attention to fads. So, more often than not, we're behind in dress style and receive only jeers and insults.

Geeks are known for academic success. I guess everybody knows that geeks are at their best when in a math or science class. Geeks just love to compute equations on their big-screened, multi-functional calculators. Science is where a geek is at home. There is so much room for open thought in science; science can always be expanded upon with theories and estimations and guesses. There's a field of study for every geek in the world: chemistry, astronomy, physics, biology, anatomy, forensics, and many others.

Geeks also have persistence. Take any average millionaire who made money with a tech business (Steve Jobs, Bill Gates), and you will find that the key elements were a strong will, a good business sense, and persistence. They had to "try, try again" to get to their goals. But they persisted. Most geeks are like that.

I guess what I'm trying to say is that being a geek is an immense advantage. Perhaps the world would be a better place to live if we all saw through the eyes of a "modified geek."—*Stephanie M.*

. . . AND I'M MORE THAN A LABEL

Last but not least, there's music preferences—another huge factor in labeling. Because of music videos, cable concerts, and TV ads, the visual images performers present have become almost as important as the music itself. When you hear that someone likes a certain type of music, you don't just hear the music in your head, you see the performers as well. You can imagine what they're wearing and how they're singing or playing. Even if you're not familiar with a certain type of music, you probably can still get a visual image because you most likely have seen similar performers on television or in magazines. Sometimes, you can recognize the artist before you've actually heard his or her music.

As a result, people tend to assume that those who *listen* to the music are like those who *make* the music. Almost every genre of music has the stereotypical spokesperson. When we think of polka music, we may see a nerd in suspenders. When we think of hip-hop or rap, we may see a thug with baggy jeans and a mean attitude. Pop music may make us picture a giddy teenybopper wearing a boy-band T-shirt and glitter barrettes.

"People often call me a goth because, in the past, people labeled goths as black-wearing, black-haired freaks. I wear black sometimes. They call me a freak because they don't dress the same way I do, and they're just scared to. They call me a raver because I dress like a person who would attend raves regularly or party hard, and I like heavy rock. They call me punk because I like hard rock, and play hard rock, and dress punkish. They call me hippie because I love sixties music, love Woodstock, and wear pants that resemble bellbottoms."—Guy, 13

Someone who listens to punk must *be* a punk, right? And all goths must be troubled kids who listen to Marilyn Manson. These are the assumptions that get made, whether they're based on reality or not.

Because there's an expected audience for certain types of music, you could also be labeled if you look obviously *different* than that audience typically does. The most common label that's associated with being different from the typical audience is wannabe: a rock wannabe, a hip-hop wannabe, a punk wannabe. This is someone who claims to like the music but doesn't seem to "get" the social culture that goes along with it.

It's not just the type of music you *listen to* that can inspire a label but also the type of music that you may *play*. Many high schools have a band or an orchestra, or some sort of music program. Teens involved in these activities ("bandies," "band geeks," or "band-aids") are labeled in an entirely different way than teens who start their *own* bands.

Apparently, it's considered cool to be a rocker in your own band because (a) you're already at least a local celebrity as soon as you play your first gig, (b) you've chosen to put together your own band so you're independent, and (c) you seem to be deep, rebellious, sensitive, hardcore, or whatever adjective makes the fans faint. Being in the school band doesn't seem to have the same cool factor because it's a *school* activity. Usually, *teachers* choose the music for school bands—and besides, when's the last time you saw a French horn player on MTV? (Of course, if you're really a devoted musician, you could join both types of bands.) Isn't it interesting to think about the different labels associated with those who are "in band" versus those who are "in *a* band"?

See how ridiculous some labels can be?

#3 Behavior/Personality

In high school, every little thing you say or do could be used to create a whole new reputation for you. That's exactly what high school feels like at times.

Once people are able to get beyond your appearance, they tend to look at your personality for clues about who you are. Your personality is a reflection of your character traits, interests, habits, and values. As with any other factor that leads to labeling, a certain personality trait doesn't mean the same thing to every person. For example, a girl who's reserved could be seen as either a prude or a tease, depending on the labeler's point of view. A guy who's naturally flirtatious may be called a player because he gives special attention to nearly every girl he meets, or he simply may be thought of as a nice guy. When someone's attitude suggests they don't care about what their peers think, they may be labeled as a loner or a freak—or seen as more of an individual.

Unfortunately, any type of nonconformity in someone's looks, attitude, or behavior can lead to a label because people tend to focus on obvious differences between themselves and others. Does this mean nonconformity is a bad thing? Not necessarily. Think about whether you're being true to yourself and your individuality.

I happen to think that being yourself shows great confidence. (Read more about individuality and confidence in Chapter 7, How to Help Yourself," on pages 110–123.)

Another influence in labeling is how someone talks. Have you ever thought about the way you speak or what words you often use? Do you have an accent? Do you say "wicked" or "dude" or "like" after every other word? And if you do, does that automatically mean you're a surferchick or surferdude? Or maybe you're into "chillin" with your "peeps" and hoping to make it to the next "partay"? If so, you may be called a homie-g. Of course, these are all words that sneak into teen vernacular everywhere. For example, I've heard people who are known as preps say, "Like, I was chillin' last night." So, as with other factors that lead to labeling, things aren't always as they seem.

> "I was labeled because I'm in all the school plays and because I'm my own person. I do what I please and think appropriate. People may have called me a freak because sometimes I do things outside of what others expect."—Girl, 16

What you do—or at least what people *think* you do—can also play a huge role in how you might be labeled. This is especially true when it comes to choices you make about behaviors that are against the rules or illegal.

For example, at your school, the term may be "cutting," "ditching," or "skipping," but they all mean not going to class. You might think it's no one's business whether you cut class. But when you don't show up, others are free to create their own scenarios about where you are (smoking behind the handball wall or making out with someone in a car). Usually, their assumptions aren't friendly. They may start calling you a stoner or a slut based on their own theories of what you do when you're not where you're supposed to be. Even if you ditch class to study for a test you have later that afternoon, people might guess that you're doing something worse.

On the flip side, if you never cut class at all—especially if you go to a school where cutting is considered "normal"—you could be branded as a major dork or goody-goody. The assumption is that you care about the rules so much that you won't risk getting in trouble even once. This may make other people think that you're boring, a quality typically associated with the nerd and goody-goody labels. It all depends on the attitude at your school. If your school is very strict, students may never dare to *think* about cutting.

"My labels seem to connect with my morals. That is, what I will and will not do."—Guy, 16

Other risky habits like using alcohol and drugs also can play a big role in the labeling game. Many teens assume that they can control their habits and stop using drugs or drinking alcohol whenever they want to. They may even consider these activities to be harmless when they're done with a group of friends or at a party. But when someone becomes dependent on these substances and uses them without the company of friends, labels such as loser, scrub, and stoner may get started. At some schools, entire groups of friends may be labeled as stoners (variations are "druggies" and "burnouts") if they're known for—or at least suspected of—using drugs a lot.

One label that's almost always linked to drugs is raver (the plural is raverz). Rave culture began in the 1980s and is now known worldwide. Raves are huge parties, usually held in the darkness of abandoned buildings, where techno music is played on booming stereo systems. Raverz often wear wide-bottom pants and protest shirts, and are known for accessorizing with glitter, glow-sticks, and baby pacifiers. But the accessory most often associated with raverz is E (short for Ecstasy, another name for the drug MDMA, which is part hallucinogen and part stimulant).

As with any other label, raver has its controversy. People who consider themselves to be raverz are sharply divided over the drug issue. Some go to raves just for the music and dancing, and say they don't need the drugs to have a good time. Others definitely are into drinking or the drug scene. They use accessories

"I felt people misunderstood what my label meant. Raver does not equal sex and drugs!"—Girl, 15

like glow-sticks and pacifiers not just for self-expression but to increase Ecstasy's effects. The use of drugs like E can lead to sexual experimentation, too. Does this mean all raverz are into these behaviors? Not necessarily. But it's easy to see why drug use has become associated with this label when there have been so many news reports about E and rave culture.

Straight-edge, on the other hand, is a label that characterizes people for actions they *don't* take. The name straight-edge comes from a music movement launched by the song "Straight Edge" by a band out of Washington, D.C., called Minor Threat; the label usually characterizes teens who are into rock music but abstain from drugs, sex, and alcohol. It's a label that these teens proudly accept, but as with any label, there are those who may use it with a totally different meaning in mind. Some teens, for example, may say they're straight-edge because they like the music scene, but they still smoke pot or drink beer.

So, behavior can lead to labels. But behavior can also *mislead* you about labels. How can it do both? It's simple. Every person is unique. There's no way that everyone who shares the same label will act the exact same way. To meet one freak is *not* to have met them all. So the next time you hear that someone is a total prude, or is heavily into drugs, or has an attitude problem—and is labeled for it—consider the fact that labels are often based on rumors and hearsay. Then find out for yourself whether this is someone you want to get to know.

#4 Grades/Intellect

Good grades are a nerd's best friends—*everyone* knows that, right? And nerds are smart but unpopular. On the other hand, ditzes and cheerleaders are dumb; they don't make good grades because they're much more concerned about their looks and popularity. Ditzes and nerds will never speak the same language—according to all of these (faulty!) assumptions. Have you ever wondered why smart is often perceived as a synonym for uncool, or why people insist on believing that cheerleaders are totally vapid?

Certain labels are associated with intelligence or a lack thereof. It's common knowledge that nerd (variation: dork) is a label given to those who take their studies seriously. Over the years, nerds have been portrayed as weak in every way except intellect. The higher your grades, the bigger the nerd you supposedly are. How come, in our society, people who play sports or who achieve in the looks department are the ones who seem to get the most admiration? Why are teens who study hard and make good grades often teased, ignored, or even hated?

> "I'm smart and put a lot of effort and time into my work. That's why I'm a nerd. I go to a good school where you have to work hard. I don't use drugs or rebel or anything, so I'm a goody-goody."
> —Girl, 16

Students who want to get high grades and ask for extra credit often are slapped with the name teacher's pet. Or they're perceived as thinking of themselves as too good for everyone else, earning the goody-goody label. Nerds are often portrayed as socially clueless, too—as if improving your intelligence means you can't find the time to interact with anything but a textbook. In some circles, nerds are even treated as complete outcasts, as if they don't deserve any notice or respect whatsoever.

In reality, having good grades doesn't mean you're antisocial. And not only nerds get good grades. Athletes often have to maintain certain grades to remain on the team (therefore many jocks earn high grades, too). Parents of all kinds of teens—who have all kinds of labels—put pressure on their kids to do well in school. Anyone who's goal-oriented has a chance to do well in school. Having goals is admirable and can lead to success in life.

> "You would think being smart would earn some respect, but it never gained much for me—at least not from the people who never care about school until the last minute and need to copy my homework, if you know what I mean."—Girl, 16

Now for the other side of the coin, or in this case, cafeteria.

Why are labels like ditz, teen queen, or cheerleader associated with inferior intelligence? For one thing, there's a stereotype that says brains and beauty can't coexist. Girls who are considered attractive are often viewed as having one-track minds, with a focus on fashion, shopping, or flirting. People assume these activities are all that can fit into these girls' brains. The reverse of this stereotype is that smart girls are plain or ugly. Of course, these stereotypes are as silly as the ones for nerds.

Another assumption is that an activity like cheerleading is dumb and so are the people who participate in it. But why is this activity dumber than other sports and interests? Is it because cheerleaders have to cheer with smiles on their faces and convey a bouncy attitude to the fans? Maybe it doesn't make sense to look happy when there's a serious sports game happening. For some people, smiling faces and cheering suggest a lack of intellect because, after all, how could someone so happy know the facts about the Vietnam War or nuclear physics? Then there are the people who simply hate sports. To them, cheerleaders may seem less than brainy because they're cheering for stupid sports.

> "I was labeled a cheerleader—meaning the stereotypical ditzy type. I have blond hair so I get a lot of labeling from that."—Girl, 16

But wait. To believe that cheerleaders are stupid, you'd have to ignore all the mental concentration and aptitude it takes to complete a gymnastics routine. You'd also have to ignore the fact that many cheerleaders earn high grades, graduate at the top of their class, and go on to good colleges. That's why these simplifications don't work.

#5 Friends

How many times have you had to say, "That's my friends, not me"? I know I've had to say it when people have made snap judgments about me based on my friends. It's not that my friends are so awful that I have to set myself apart from them—it's that sometimes people forget too quickly that a friendship doesn't mean a shared identity. Just because people are friends doesn't mean they all like the same things, behave the same way, or dress alike. I'd never dress the way some of my friends do. We all have our different styles, our different personalities, our different *selves.*

When you see friends together, it's natural to assume that they have many similarities. After all, they're friends. Friends support and influence each other. Knowing this, you might guess that if you don't like one person in a certain group, you won't like any of that person's friends either. But this isn't always the case. Friends don't share the same exact personalities or viewpoints. They can agree to disagree and to respect each other's opinions. You can't assume that everyone in a certain group thinks and acts the same way.

When you see each person as an individual, instead of as a faceless member of a group, you're more likely to realize that you can't label everyone the same way. After all, what if one member of the group "fits" a certain label more than the others? Do you then describe that person as the "preppier prep standing by that other prep"? Or the "freakiest freak over there by the sort of freaky freak"? How silly does that sound?

Here's where it gets tricky: Some groups seem to *like* to be defined by their similarities. Remember how I said that a friendship doesn't mean a shared identity? The exception to this rule is cliques. In the Teen Labels Survey, teens were asked to talk about their experiences with cliques. Many of them said that, at their schools, cliques and labels go hand in hand. There's often a jock clique, a prep clique, and so on—but this doesn't mean that all jocks or all preps are part of a clique.

Cliques aren't the same as friendships, although you can be friends with people in your clique. Sound confusing? It is. A group of friends are the people you hang out with most of the time, but not *exclusively.* You're not attached at the hip. Cliques are different because they're exclusive. There are rules (spoken or unspoken) about sticking together and not letting outsiders in.

Is this description upsetting? You may be thinking that you and your friends aren't like this. Great! Maybe you're not a clique. For the purposes of this book, clique will take on a negative vibe. You may disagree with this if clique means something good to you. Among the teens who were surveyed, cliques often were seen as a negative thing, and I agree with those opinions.

How do you define a clique?

"A group of people who think they're better than others."—*Guy, 15*

"A group that is closed off from other types of people and is selective about the types of people it associates with."—*Girl, 15*

"A clique is a group that sometimes excludes others— they might not know they are doing it, but they do." —*Guy, 16*

"A group of friends that is inward thinking (not working with or treating people outside the ring of friends the same)."—*Guy, 16*

"An exclusive bunch of people who hate people different than themselves."—*Girl, 16*

"Cliques are a way to single people out who are different—to be mean and make people feel bad about themselves."—*Girl, 15*

"People who don't like others out of their 'circle' because they think poorly of them without getting to know them."—*Girl, 16*

"A group of people who think they're superior to every-one else."—*Guy, 16*

"A group of 'friends' who don't really CARE about how people feel and who don't let anyone in who either isn't pretty or who doesn't get enjoyment out of making fun of others."—*Girl, 17*

"Everyone in a clique is very into each other. Secluded from everyone else."—*Girl, 17*

"A group of people who think they dominate and are the majority."—*Guy, 16*

"The same people hanging out every day and sitting together every single day."—*Girl, 15*

"People who are *not* universal, not able to get to know different people who aren't interested in exactly everything they are."—*Girl, 15*

"A group of people who are friends and who, if someone tries to talk to them, will all bash them (talk about them) after they leave, or else tell them to leave."—*Girl, 16*

"A group of people who run in the same circles whose radii don't change."—*Guy, 16*

Cliques have a few characteristics in common:

1. Conformity. Everyone in the clique generally wears the same type of clothes, talks the same ("Yo, yo, baby," or "like, whatever, you know"), and likes the same people. Crushes on others outside the group usually aren't allowed.

2. Leaders. There's often one person (or a mini group of people) clearly seen as being in charge. The One In Charge sets the standards and has the power to make others behave a certain way or be dismissed from the clique.

3. Restriction of members. Only certain people can get into the clique. The people who are chosen are a lot like the people who are already in the clique.

4. It's a friendship, but . . . People in the clique may be best friends, but the fact that they're in the clique plays a key role in their friendship. It's kind of a chicken and egg situation. Which came first—the clique, the labels, or the friendships?

The people had the same label, so they became friends? They *were* friends and so they were labeled the same way? Or maybe they only like each other because they're in the same clique? It varies from case to case, but either way, it can be harmful—especially when one friend dumps another for not following clique rules.

5. An attitude of superiority. You know, "Ha ha, you're different, so we'll make fun of you." What's *that* all about? A friend of mine actually had to stop a clique of girls from teasing a boy who had a speech impediment. Not all cliques and clique members are this immature, and not all of them tease others. However, there's definitely a mentality of there's "power in numbers" when it comes to cliques.

If you're on the outside looking in at a clique, do you feel any warm and fuzzy feelings toward those people? Probably not. Chances are, you see clique members who seem to look, act, walk, talk, and feel the same. If those people project an attitude of superiority and snub you, you're obviously not going to think of them in a good way. This is why it's easy to label people who are in a clique. First, they seem to *want* their label (conformity, remember?). Second, they seem to *deserve* to be labeled since they're not very nice to those outside the group.

This brings me back to my original point in this book: People are more than their labels. Even though I don't think cliques are positive, I still believe that clique members deserve to be treated as individuals. Think about it this way: Suppose your best friend has an annoying trait, like spreading rumors or bragging about grades. Now, imagine if every person in your high school thought *you* had that same characteristic, just because your friend does. What if others never bothered to look beyond your friend, or the other people you hang out with, to see the real you? Consider that whenever you're about to label someone based on who they hang out with.

It's amazing how many things can lead to a label you don't want: a different haircut, some tight pants, a protest button, a science award, a new friend, or even a rumor about something you've supposedly done. The assumptions that people may make, and the labels they may put on you, can be annoying and very confusing. You probably know that there's much more to you than what people see on the surface. That's true of others as well. Keep reminding yourself that everyone you encounter deserves as much of a chance as you do to be seen as more than a label.

TRY IT!

Think of all the labels that are used in your school. Now, take out a sheet of paper. Using a pen or pencil, divide the paper into five columns. Pick a label to focus on and write it at the top of the page; then write each one of the five factors (see pages 27–46) above each column. Inside each column, describe how each factor ties into the label. Do you agree or disagree with the stereotypes the labels suggest? Are *you* labeled? If so, can you think of anything from the five factors that might contribute to the way you're labeled?

Part 2
HOW LABELS MAKE PEOPLE FEEL

Do labels affect you? My guess is yes. Do they affect you in a good or bad way? That's up for debate. I included this quiz to get you thinking about how labels are used at your school and how you feel about them.

Read the following questions and see if they're generally true for you:

1. Do people judge you because of your label?

2. Do you judge others based on their labels?

3. Do you get made fun of because of a label you've been given?

4. At school, is there a social ladder based on labels?

5. Do you feel that you can't be friends with, hang out with, or go out with anyone—that it's an unspoken rule that you stay with your "own kind"?

6. Are people's reputations at school based on their labels?

7. Do certain groups or cliques avoid each other?

8. Does your school have cliques that are highly exclusive?

9. Do labels help tell you if someone is considered cool or not?

Did you answer yes to most, if not all, of these questions? If so, you wouldn't be the first. No matter what kind of school you go to, the students probably use labels as a way to categorize people.

When you categorize people, you start to make assumptions about them—the smart ones, the stupid ones, the cool ones, the ones most (or least) likely to succeed. In the process, you may forget a few important things. People can rise above your expectations. They can sink down to your low expectations. They can do things you never imagined they'd do.

In Part 2, you'll find out about the many different ways labeling has made other teens feel: pleased or confused; recognized or rejected; popular or unpopular; misunderstood or miserable. Somewhere in here, you're bound to recognize the way you've felt, too.

CHAPTER 3

Labels: A Social Boost?

"I was called that stuff because I try to be that stuff."
From the Teen Labels Survey

When I first started researching labels and their effects, I met a teen named Melissa online. She had this to say: "I am labeled popular at my school, and I think it's very hard to be popular. You have to keep up a reputation like 'I am popular and better than you.' I wish it could be different because it makes me feel bad when I am mean to other teens. I don't understand why we are so mean to the nerds or the other teens who don't hang out with us. I guess I do it because everybody else does it. I wish I could stop, but I still want to stay popular. It's the thing I thrive on." Melissa isn't the only teen who feels this way. Some teens are so eager to fit in with a certain group, or to maintain a reputation, that they'll put on an act every single day.

We all present ourselves in different ways when we're in the company of different people—but this isn't the same as putting on an act. For example, you don't talk to a teacher the same way you talk to your best friend. At times, it's natural to be more (or less) polite, casual, or friendly depending on who it is you're talking to. Everyone does it.

But what if people . . .

- behave a certain way to be accepted, be popular, or fit a label?

- feel as if they're following a set of social rules that governs their every thought and move?

- can't be themselves because they don't trust that being themselves is good enough?

- use labeling to make themselves feel better by making other people feel *worse?*
- think their label defines them above anything else?

The answers to these questions aren't as easy as 1-2-3. In the Teen Labels Survey, many teens talked about how they *like* their labels and actually *chose them* for themselves. It's true that labels can help some teens feel more special, popular, or noticed. Labels, in some ways, can actually boost people up.

When Asked...

How did you feel about the label(s) you were given?

Teens Answered...

"Proud because people acknowledge my intelligence, my strength, or my sporting abilities. Besides, nobody makes fun of me with these labels. They're only words."—*Guy, 15*

"They rock, labels on people are sweet—they hold together society."—*Guy, 15*

"Some I love!"—*Girl, 16*

"I *am* those labels, therefore guilty as charged."—*Guy, 16*

"It's my friends who say them, so it doesn't bother me. I've actually embraced most of my labels and nick-names."—*Girl, 15*

"It was cool because they thought I was cool."—*Guy, 14*

"Good, because that's what I was going for."—*Guy, 15*

"I did not feel bad because I am open-minded about what people say. Also, I like the labels."—*Guy, 16*

"They were cool, so I was flattered. I *go* for being like that, it's my goal."—*Girl, 15*

"They didn't bother me, because they're for the most part true."—*Girl, 15*

"I feel okay, because I earned them."—*Guy, 18*

"Being called a preppy wasn't really bad. It was more like a compliment than an insult."—*Guy, 15*

"I don't mind labels. I make myself what I am, and I'm proud of it."—*Guy, 15*

"We all put out the 'vibe,' so to say, and then we are labeled how we *want* to be labeled."—*Guy, 17*

"I think that labeling is a good thing because it gives you a sense of belonging to a group and a sense that you have other people looking out for you in tough times (because they . . . are like you)."—*Guy, 13*

When reading these quotes, did you notice that more guys than girls felt fine about their labels? This was true on the surveys in general. To learn more, check out Chapter 5, "Guy vs. Girl Labeling" on pages 80–90.

If a label can boost you up, then is labeling a *positive* thing? At first, you might think so. But wait just a moment. If you look at the underlying motives, you might realize that some teens use labels because they want to be or stay popular (like Melissa described). Other teens may use labels to fit into or be accepted by a clique. And still others may see their label as ultimate proof that they're cool—or at least *somebody.*

These motives are closely tied to popularity and peer pressure, two major aspects of the high school social scene. If this is the case, are labels truly a positive thing? You can decide for yourself.

Popularity

On the Teen Labels Survey, teens were asked which labels were most associated with popular or unpopular people. While labels can mean different things at different schools, there were some common answers to the question. Do the following statements surprise you or not, based on what goes on at your school?

1. Labels like cheerleader, jock, prep, thug, homie-g, and hip-hopper tend to describe people who are popular.

2. Labels like goth, geek, punk, loner, goody-goody, and freak tend to describe people who aren't.

Maybe your school's social ladder reflects these trends. Or maybe you totally disagree with what some of the survey respondents had to say. No two schools are the same. And you're entitled to your opinion.

Isn't it interesting, however, that certain social factors are considered more acceptable than others? Think about the five factors of labeling (see pages 27–46) and how they connect to popularity in high school. On a very general level (remember, we're talking stereotypes and simplifications here), being preppy and athletic seems to rate people higher on the so-called popularity scale. Being smart and/or following the rules usually ranks lower. Looking obviously different—for example, goth or punk—tends to mark people as outsiders (which may be just fine by them). Membership in a clique, on the other hand, may identify people as insiders.

"Labeling can be good when you use labels in good ways (prep, jock). It can really make people happy and help them feel good about themselves. For the most part, I think labeling is very helpful and sometimes very motivating!"—Girl, 13

Do you ever wonder why certain people are popular while others aren't? It's not as if popular people have signs on their heads saying "I'm cool." Yet, it quickly becomes clear in any school who's considered cool and who's not. There's almost always a social ladder of some sort, with people on the top and the bottom. Even if you were to move to a new school, you'd be able to pick out the popular people based on how others treat them. The popular people might even have labels that are totally different from the ones that the popular people at your other school had, but you'd still be able to tell who's considered cool.

Popular has become a synonym for cool in many high schools. Sometimes, the popular people aren't that well liked—they

"I never want to be popular. Most popular kids at my school are mean to kids who aren't popular, and it makes kids feel so bad. I'd rather do things I enjoy and not have to worry about 'Is this cool, is this okay, will people talk about me tomorrow at school, will people whisper about me behind my back?' Sorry, I would never want to have to deal with that."—Girl, 13

may even be hated, especially if they're part of a powerful clique. Yet, the popular people are accepted as a symbol of being cool. Have you ever been jealous of a popular person? If not, I'm guessing you know someone who has been. Maybe you've been intimidated by someone who's popular? Intimidation may earn someone an uncontested nomination for homecoming king/queen, but this doesn't mean everyone in the school actually *likes* the person.

Knowing what you now know about popularity, do you think it's important to be popular? Popularity doesn't guarantee that you'll be liked. While you may become cool, this doesn't mean you'll automatically be happy. Plus, if you base your happiness on the fact that you're considered cool, one negative comment from someone who's more popular or even someone who isn't popular could break the foundation of your happiness. That's fragile ground.

"If I ran for school president and my plans were 10 BILLION times better than a prep's, the prep would win by a landslide because kids don't judge people on their views, but on how 'cool' you are."
—Guy, 17

Popularity is associated with being cool, but you can definitely be a cool person and not be in the popular crowd. Being cool is actually more about individuality than conformity. Your unique talents could make you popular without your even knowing it. Are you funny? Are you a good writer? Are you kind? Are you smart? Are you an artist? People might already think you're cool just because you're unique in some way. If you're a true individual and you respect yourself, you're cool.

Maybe you have labeled people to try to make yourself appear more cool, popular, or attractive. If so, you're not alone. Just as some bullies will beat up others to make themselves feel more powerful, some high school students will label others to make themselves feel more socially acceptable.

"Why do people label others? Because people need some way to reassure themselves that they are better than someone else."—Girl, 13

They try to divert negative attention away from themselves by any means necessary, even by saying, "Look at the scrub over there!" (As in, since I've noticed the scrub, I can't *possibly* be one myself. Plus, scrubs wouldn't label other scrubs as scrubs, right?)

Other people usually see through this behavior. Besides, do you really gain anything from it? You're still the same you, except that you label people. Labeling others might actually make people more inclined to label you. You get what you give, if you know what I mean.

Peer Pressure

Peer pressure. We all know what it is. We've all felt it or heard about its effects. I'm sure you've felt the pressure, or pressured someone else, at least once in your life.

Labeling is actually a type of peer pressure. When you label, you assign someone an identity—you tell that person who he is or should be. By calling someone a word that isn't his name, you show him and everyone else that you're defining him the way *you* want to.

If you do this, you're using labels to "put people in their place"—in this case, their place on the social ladder of your school. Their position plays a role in how they're treated. Are they liked? Ignored? Admired? Avoided?

Did you ever imagine a label could be that influential? Suppose you call some girl a skank. You know exactly what skank implies and the social effects it could have. Using one simple but powerful word, you show her what your opinion of her is. Spreading and repeating the label is a form of pressure—and a constant reminder that the person isn't cool enough or good enough.

"Labeling kind of helps you establish your position in society. It helps you make yourself better."—Guy, 16

Trying to change someone's sense of self or the way others think of her can make you feel important—temporarily. But it's just a power trip. Later, you may actually feel pretty bad about how you treated the person.

Maybe you use labels to help define where *you* belong on the social ladder. Like other people, you probably want to know if, and where, you fit in. In high school, there's a lot of pressure to be a part of some kind of group, whether it's a group of friends or a clique (for more on the differences between them, see pages 42–46). To fit in, you may try to associate yourself with a label by getting other people to see that you have the characteristics that go along with the label. Once you're part of a group or a clique, the label you share with the other people in it starts to define who you and your friends are.

Sometimes, there's so much pressure to get into a clique that you might change your entire look and behavior to fit in. If this hasn't happened to you, it's probably happened to a friend of yours or *someone* you go to school with. Maybe you've watched as someone you know starts wearing different clothes or starts drinking alcohol as a way to fit in. Perhaps you've seen someone become more popular and start to treat others (maybe even former friends) with new disdain. Over time, the person practically becomes someone else—someone you barely recognize anymore. The pressure to fit a label or stay in a clique can

"People feel like they need a label for an identity, because they don't know who they are or what they are going to do."—Girl, 14

"Once, I had a friend who was really nice but she was kind of a dork. My friends started to make fun of her cause of how she looked, how much popularity she had, how many friends she had, and what she wore. I joined in cause I didn't want to feel left out. I started to not talk to her cause if anyone really popular saw me with her they would immediately label me as a dork. I didn't want that, so I stopped being friends with her. I wish that labels had not stopped our friendship cause she was a really good friend."—Girl, 13

be so powerful that the person forgets how to act any other way.

Sometimes, no matter what you do, you can't find a way to fit in with any group. If this happens, is this some kind of reflection on you? I suppose that's possible. Though more likely, it's a reflection of the social problems and pressures that exist at most high schools. There's pressure to fit in but also pressure to *exclude*. This means, inevitably, that some people are left out. This isn't fair—and neither is labeling. That's why it's so important to consider the negative effects that labels can have.

I WAS LABELED, TOO. . . .

Ever since I can remember, I was labeled. I spent many years in a private Catholic school where I was the youngest student. I had brown hair, not blond. I had freckles, not a tan. I was tall, not average. I wasn't skinny like the other girls. I remember being six years old and asking my mom why the kids made fun of me. Why they laughed while I cried. Why they thought it was fun to say so many hurtful things. To this day, I still don't understand.

I thought that as people grew older, they also grew wiser. That's not always the case. I transferred to a public school in ninth grade. I learned that no matter where you go, or what you do, people are still the same. On the first day of school, I introduced myself to some girls, only to have them laugh at me and walk away. They said I was stuck up—a Catholic school brat. They called me smarty, musician, athlete—anything to lower my self-esteem and raise theirs. Little did they know, I was just a shy new kid, trying to make some new friends. They never gave me a chance.

However, a girl named Mary did give me a chance. Mary is an extremely talented artist and lives a very exciting life. She also dresses in all black and dyes her hair crazy colors. People find this to be disturbing, weird, and "not normal." People have called her Scary Mary. In truth, Mary is probably the most gentle, kind-hearted, sweet person I will ever meet. People just made assumptions about her because of the way she acted and dressed. They didn't try to see who she really was. I consider myself lucky to be her friend.

I guess, over the past few years, I've become more and more aware of labeling. I go to a school that has a very colorful selection of people. There are white people and black people. Some are gay, and some are straight. Some play sports, while some are studious. Everyone is different. And you know what? It doesn't matter. Difference is what makes the world so wonderful.—*Laurie H.*

`. . . AND I'M MORE THAN A LABEL`

Reality Check

Popularity and peer pressure are links in the same chain. They're so connected that it's hard to tell where one ends and the other begins.

In some ways, it may seem as if we're all miserable in high school because of these social pressures. Well, high school isn't *all* bad. Some of the pressures really do take a toll, though. Do you ever wonder: If you're miserable anyway, wouldn't it be better if you were a miserable *popular* person? At least you'd have your popularity to look forward to each day.

It might seem as if popularity has its perks—on the surface. But there's a downside to everything. While you may be able to explain away any insecurities or a lack of self-confidence with "At least I'm still popular," you also have to live in constant anticipation of the day when you might not be popular anymore. Believe it or not, this fear can leave some teens feeling even more miserable than their not-so-popular peers. If you desperately want to be popular and fit in because you want to be liked or admired, you're heading down the wrong road. Popularity isn't some magical path to happiness.

Here's a question for you. Is it okay to label a popular person? Your answer should be the same as it is for any other person. I hope your answer is no. Somehow, it may seem as if being popular or being part of a clique makes people fair targets. After all, they treat others as inferiors, just to make themselves feel more superior, so they deserve what they get—or so the reasoning goes. The labeling game can be played both ways.

Is this fair, though? People who are seen as popular are still *people*—they have problems, and more importantly, *feelings* just like everyone else. Talking about that "snobby cheerleader" behind her back is no better than talking about that "annoying freak." It's just not right to use people for an ego trip.

Maybe if we all took a moment to think about how the other person might feel before we use a label, school would be easier for everyone. Well, everyone except freshmen—they've got it rough regardless.

Instead of focusing on popularity or the pressure to fit in, take satisfaction in being popular among your own friends. I know it's not easy to deal with the other pressures. And I know that no matter how you feel about yourself when you wake up in the morning, things can change as soon as you walk through the double doors of high school and have to hear the opinions and labels. Try to keep it all in perspective. Will any of this stuff—popularity, peer pressure, who's in, who's out—matter much after you graduate and move on from high school? Not likely!

CHAPTER 4

Labels: A Social Nightmare?

"Everyone has their opinions of you. It's what makes us human.
If you let it bother you it eats you up; if it doesn't bother
you, you're denying your human side."
From the Teen Labels Survey

A couple years ago, I took a speech and debate class. We learned that there are always two sides to every argument. Labeling is no different. There's no *one* way that labeling affects teens. Everyone reacts differently. One guy may love being labeled a loner because he thinks it's cool; another guy may think the loner label means no one likes him, and feel rejected. For the most part, however, the Teen Labels Survey showed that many teens don't like being labeled. And for good reasons.

What happens when labels . . .

• prevent people from getting to know one another?

• hurt people or their reputations?

• leave people feeling rejected or left out?

• lead to feelings of anger, anxiety, or depression?

These are all negative consequences of labeling—and they affect teens every day. If you've had your social life torn apart by labels, rumors, a clique, or vicious gossip, I believe this chapter can help you. Even if your social life is fine, I think this chapter can help. You might go from liking your label to hating it as fast as you can say "misconception."

Label Radar

Label radar—it's different for every teen, but we all use it. Label radar is a personal screening process that helps us decide what types of people we'll befriend. For many reasons (how we're treated, our level of popularity, how well we fit in), we think that certain types of people won't match with us. Our label radar helps us detect who we'll be friendly toward or ignore. Label radar isn't foolproof—for anybody. To prove it, I'll tell you my own story.

Once, when I was at an academic summer session, I labeled a girl named Shelly. I thought she was a snob. To me, Shelly looked like the snobby characters I'd seen in movies and on television. I thought her facial features made her seem as if she were looking down at everyone else. Her voice even sounded snobby, and her laugh seemed fake.

During the last week of the session, everyone began to hang out in larger groups because we realized that our time together was almost over. I ended up sitting at a lunch table with Shelly, along with some mutual friends. Believe me, I was surprised we had mutual friends. As we all talked, I realized that Shelly wasn't snobby, as I had thought. I wondered if I'd misjudged her. At that moment, I understood that I'd allowed myself to be fooled by appearances and misconceptions. Then Shelly said that a lot of people in the session thought she was a snob, and that took me by surprise. I realized that other teens had labeled her, too.

I had never even met this girl or exchanged one word with her before that day. But somehow, my label radar told me not to be friends with her. I based my opinion of her—for four weeks—solely on her physical attributes and on stereotypes. As a result, I missed out on getting to know someone who was actually very nice.

Using label radar, you may screen people based on the five factors (see pages 27–46):

1. Clothing Style/Appearance

2. Interests/Activities/Music Preferences

3. Behavior/Personality

4. Grades/Intellect

5. Friends

You may also be influenced by other key factors: someone's financial background, race or ethnicity, religion, or sex. (Read more about these factors in Chapter 5, "Guy vs. Girl Labeling" on pages 80–90 and in Chapter 6, "Slurs and Other Hate Words," on pages 91–107.)

What would happen if you turned off your label radar for a day? You might get to know someone you would otherwise reject, avoid, ignore, tease, or dismiss. Why let yourself miss out on the chance to meet people—people you might have more in common with than you ever thought possible?

I LABELED SOMEONE . . .

Okay, I had eyes. There was no denying this boy was beautiful, with his short jet-black hair, athletic build, and huge, striking blue eyes. Beautiful—yes. Anything else of substance, however? No.

Eddie and I had gone to school together for years. I was the bookish, slightly sarcastic brunette who mainly stayed with the "artsy" crew in high school. Eddie was a star athlete and kind of a class heartthrob. He had girls in lower grades giggling over him, and he'd flirt back mercilessly. He was a pompous jerk. I had never had a conversation with the boy, but I knew that much about him.

We were first thrown together in the fall of our senior year in creative writing class. It was my third time taking that class; I was serious about becoming a writer, while Eddie, I assumed, was only there because his guidance counselor had to stick him somewhere. Of course, we ended up with computers next to each other. I thought to myself how entertaining this semester would be . . . I couldn't wait to see what this guy would try to pass off as poems and stories.

Our first assignment was to write about an event that had dramatically changed our lives. I immediately pumped out a few pages on how my father's death had impacted me. The way that class worked, we all put our stories into a packet and then gathered in a circle to read them out loud.

I read mine, which was sensitive and personal and from the heart. When I was done, I noticed that Eddie's story came after mine. He looked up self-consciously. "Oh, I can't follow that one," he admitted, and I rolled my eyes. Of course you can't, I thought. Because you're a moron.

But then Eddie began to read. He had written about his grandfather's death. One part especially touched me. Eddie described helping his little brother tie his tie for their grandfather's funeral, and remembered when his grandfather had helped him with his own tie on the day of his first communion.

All of a sudden, Eddie was no longer a dumb jock to me. He was sensitive, smart, and thoughtful. We formed a bond during that semester. I have always been an easy target for teasing, and Eddie knew all the right things to say, teasing me about my obsession with my long, curly hair and about the long, sappy stories I wrote. "I want to read another one of Diana's romance novels!" he'd joke.

After that class, Eddie and I went our separate ways, but there would always be a silent understanding between the two of us—the popular jock and the quiet writer. He taught me not to prejudge people. Looking back, Eddie probably had prejudged me as well, and hopefully, I taught him the same lesson.

I had placed a label on Eddie. I assumed that because he dated cheerleaders and hung out with football players, he had no good points. What I found, instead, was a boy who had a soul as beautiful as his eyes.—*Diana R.*

. . . WHO WAS MORE THAN A LABEL

Ask yourself:

- Are there people at school who barely make a blip on your radar screen? (You consider them so unimportant that you barely acknowledge their existence?)

- Do you always react a particular way toward people who have certain labels? (For example, do you automatically avoid the jocks, or dismiss the freaks, or gossip about the cheerleaders?)

- Do you pay too much attention to artificial barriers, such as race or religion? (For instance, do you only hang out with people who have a similar skin color or background to your own?)

These behaviors not only hurt others—they hurt *you*, too. By staying behind the boundaries of your radar screen, you limit your ability to get to know other people. The world is a very diverse place. You may be surprised at what you're missing!

When Asked...

How did you feel about the label(s) you were given?

Teens Answered...

"I don't appreciate labels, or any one-word summary of an entire person."—*Girl, 15*

"The labels I'm given—disabled, handicapped, physically challenged—make me feel less intelligent or 'with it,' less relatable, and less 'able' to fit in or be accepted."—*Girl, 15*

"My labels were representations of the ignorance that exists in our society, and nothing more."—*Guy, 15*

"I don't like labels, they limit people."—*Guy, 16*

"Terrible, almost killed myself."—*Girl, 17*

"Sometimes it aggravates me because it's not true, and sometimes I feel that I have to set the standard for my label—and I really can't be me!"—*Girl, 15*

"It feels annoying and hurts my feelings."—*Guy, 16*

"Perplexed, annoyed."—*Guy, 16*

"I ignored everything but slut—that one pushed me over the edge because the people saying it didn't even know me, they were just starting stuff."—*Girl, 16*

"They are mostly untrue and some are offensive."—*Girl, 16*

"It was unfair. They didn't even know me."—*Girl, 16*

"They were stupid because I only want to be labeled by my *name*."—*Guy, 15*

"Bad—labels make me feel less individualized."—*Girl, 16*

"I think that labels are stupid and degrading."—*Girl, 16*

"At first I let them bother me, but then I realized that they were, after all, just labels. It is up to me to decide who I am, not others."—*Girl, 16*

"They made me look at myself and try to see what they saw. They made me very self-conscious."—*Guy, 17*

"Angry and embarrassed."—*Guy, 17*

"Not good. What gives them the right to decide who I am? But at the same time, who cares what others decide about me? It's what I feel about me that counts."—*Girl, 15*

"Bad, like no one wanted to take the time to really get to know me."—*Girl, 17*

> "It hurt me very bad. Like a dagger in my heart!"—*Guy, 15*

> "I feel extremely bad when I'm labeled, almost as if my self-esteem has been popped. I feel bad because words go very deep into your soul."—*Guy, 14*

When Labels Hurt

Most of us can guess that labels with obviously negative meanings, like slut and loser, can affect someone. These words seem to pack a bigger punch than other labels. Maybe it's because they have the potential to last longer.

For example, if you're labeled as a punk and you decide to change your image, once you start dressing differently and hanging out with different people, it's much harder for others to label you a punk. However, if you're labeled a loser and you want to get rid of your label, it's not as simple as changing friends or clothes. Labels like this one (as well as loner, nerd, skank, or freak) are based heavily on other people's perceptions of who you are. They have to believe that *you've* changed, not just that your taste in friends or clothes has changed.

How do you feel about your label? Does it make you cringe? Does it make you cry? No matter how bad it feels to be labeled, always remember not to blame yourself. You didn't do something to deserve a label—someone else probably decided to tease or provoke you with this one word. Is it fair? No. Even if you *did* do something to start the labeling, this doesn't mean you deserve to have it continue, especially if it's clear that you want it to stop.

Suppose you had a label that was totally based on lies, but people kept repeating it to you. Would you (1) give in and resign yourself to being identified by that label? Or (2) refuse to be defined by anyone else and continue to believe in yourself? Maybe you automatically said yes to number two. Well, even the strongest person can begin to doubt himself or herself once a label feels as if it's going to be around forever.

One of the nasty effects of being labeled is lowered self-respect. When you're labeled in a way that you don't want to be, you might feel as if you "deserve" this label. If it's used over a long period of time, you might even begin to act like this label. You figure, what's the point in trying to prove you're not what people think you are?

When your label and the way people treat you are hurtful, it's natural to feel upset and confused. You may wonder why you of all people had to get this type of reputation. You may feel like a social failure. You may even wrack your brain to see where you went wrong or what you did to be labeled this way. Okay, feel this way for a second, but then wake up. Keep in mind that a label is only someone's perception of you—it's not *you*. Whether the label is partially true or totally false, you have the right to be called by your NAME.

> "I hate coming to school. I'm getting Fs and Ds because I'm afraid of what people think of me. I cry because I'm always excluded. People talk about going to parties and other people's houses after school right in front of me, and I'm not invited. Anger, sadness, pressure, depression, grades, school, chores, boys, and popularity are all cramped into my heart. I don't know what to do. I feel like I'm going to explode!"—Girl, 13

Before other people will treat you well, you first have to treat yourself well. There's one opinion of you that counts more than any other—and that's *your* opinion. What do you think of yourself? Was your automatic answer something like, "I'm a loser," "I'm an idiot," "I'm totally unpopular," or "I can't stand myself"? If so, you're hurting yourself with negative self-talk.

Negative self-talk is a phrase that describes your "inner critic" or that annoying voice in your head. It's basically a way to beat yourself up every day. Negative self-talk hurts you. You wouldn't want some other person going around talking to you like that all the time, saying you're dumb or hopeless. Even if you would take verbal abuse from someone else, would you enjoy it? You'd probably be upset at the person for not showing you respect.

Negative self-talk can hurt you even more than a label can. That's because when someone else says something bad about you, you can tell yourself it isn't true. When you're mean to yourself, though, there's no one to defend you.

I learned this the hard way. Whenever I was nervous, I talked a lot to hide the fact that I was uncomfortable. (FYI: Rambling on when one is nervous is not a good idea.) I said some things that weren't exactly brainy or well thought out. Then I'd try to laugh it off, and I'd say to myself—and out loud—"I'm such a ditz." I was actually at the top of my class and very smart, but at those moments, I felt so stupid.

I should have known it would happen eventually: After calling myself a ditz for about a year, I heard that some guy had been calling me a ditz behind my back. Ouch! That hurt. But you know what hurt more? I knew I was the one to blame, and that really annoyed me. I had told myself I was a ditz, even though I knew it wasn't true. And I'd put out an image of myself as a ditz for so long, what did I think would happen? Despite the evidence that I was smart, people paid attention to what I thought of myself.

> When you call yourself an idiot, ditz, loser, or other negative name, you place a label on yourself.

Why did I say I was a ditz? Part of me actually wanted to make others feel more comfortable. I thought people would like me more if they thought I wasn't a "brain." Have you ever bonded with someone over getting a bad grade? In some ways, teen misery loves company. And somehow, in our society, being smart is often perceived as uncool. I wanted to fit in. After a while, it became second nature for me to say I was a ditz; sometimes I'd even say I was an idiot. I barely noticed when I mentioned it, but the people around me must have.

The way you talk *to* yourself and *about* yourself can affect how you and others think of you. If you want to change how others think of you, change how you think of yourself. Listen to your self-talk. Some negative words to look out for include: *never, can't,* and *no one.* Words like these are too final. They don't leave room for exceptions, and they make a situation seem much worse than it really is.

Replace negative self-talk with positive words that help you feel more powerful and in charge of your life. Instead of "I'm an idiot," tell yourself, "I made a mistake, I learned from it, and now I'm moving on." Instead of saying, "I'll always be this label, so what's the point in trying," it's better for your self-image to say, "I have changed. I am more than a label, even if others don't see it. Who cares what they think?" This is an easy first step toward change.

Once you start showing respect for yourself on the inside, it will show on the outside. You'll feel more proud of yourself. You'll walk with your head held higher. You'll be more able to look people in the eye or smile because you'll know you deserve respect. Self-respect can lead to greater self-confidence. (You can read more about confidence in Chapter 7, "How to Help Yourself," on pages 110–123.)

I can't promise you what some self-help books do, such as a better you in just two weeks! However, I can tell you that self-respect—and the confidence it can lead to—is a natural high. It's not a magic wand, and it won't turn your situation into something picture-perfect. It *will* help you deal with the situation and realize that there are other things in life to focus your valuable energy on.

When Labels Alienate

Do you remember playing the Telephone game in elementary school? The object of the game was to whisper a message from the first person to the last person in a group, and then see if the message stayed the same. The message always changed, and the more players there were, the stranger the message became. For example, someone would start with, "I only eat yellow bananas for dinner." By the time the message got to the end of the chain, the last person would say something totally different like, "Hannah is selling paint thinner."

Isn't this how gossip travels? It goes from one ear to the next, with no guarantee that the final message will be anything like the original one. As the chain of gossip grows, the information becomes less and less true and usually more and more cruel, scandalous, and reputation damaging. When we played Telephone, there was often one person who would change the message on purpose. In the same way, a person can use gossip and rumors to sway people's opinions of someone else.

Gossip is one way that labels can get started and spread around. ("Oh, I heard he's such a player." Or "My brother went out with her and she is so altie, it's scary.") Sometimes, these bits of information start off innocently but quickly turn nasty. At other times, the person spreading the rumor, gossip, or label has bad intentions and *wants* to turn another person into a target. Having knowledge of others (even if it isn't true) can make some people feel powerful or superior. If you're a victim of this kind of thing, you know how alienating it can be to have other people talking about you behind your back or saying mean things to your face. (For tips on stopping gossip, see pages 118–119.)

> "Labels are wrong! What about the 'Geek Table'? I mean, come on. Those poor people who get called geeks, nerds, weird, different—it's plain mean. It is. It is! What would you say or think if you were called that?"—Girl, 13

Why do teens behave this way? I'm not an expert on behavior, but I think people act like this to feel more popular or because of peer pressure. (You can read more about popularity and peer pressure in Chapter 3, "Labels: A Social Boost?" on pages 53–58.) Some people seem to enjoy making others feel singled out, alienated, or inferior. Calling someone a geek, nerd, loser, freak, or slut is a way to shut him or her out, while leaving the person open to all sorts of teasing and gossip. For some people, treating others this way is almost like a game—but it's not harmless, like a game of Telephone.

One of my goals for this book was to open people's eyes to how others may feel. Have you been picked on because of a label, or been a victim of gossip and rumors? If so, you know how it hurts. If you're someone who participates in this behavior, you may think it's harmless or that the people you pick on somehow deserve it. The truth is, they don't deserve it. Put yourself in their shoes and think about how this might feel.

If school is a social nightmare for you and you're being mis-
treated, you're probably feeling really frustrated and stressed out.
All teens have stress, but you may have more than your fair share
if you're constantly worrying about what people think of you. I
understand that other people's words can be hurtful, and I also
know what it's like to want everyone to like you. This isn't necessarily bad. But when people's words and opinions cause you a lot
of stress, it's time to make changes. Stress can lead to health problems like tension headaches and fatigue, making it harder to focus
on school, grades, and activities that are important to you.

If dealing with your label and trying to fit in have become a
burden in your life, talk to someone you trust before you're
affected any further. You can talk to your friends, if that helps. You
can also talk to a trusted adult, like a parent, teacher, or school
counselor. Holding in your feelings and problems tends to make
them worse. Talking is a good way to let things out.

TRY IT!

Don't ever forget about the healing effects of writing. Write down how you feel when you're labeled, teased, or gossiped about. Write about everything that's bothering you. You can even write a letter to the person who labels you the most—but don't send it. The simple act of writing down how you really feel can give you back a sense of control. Tear up the letter afterward and throw it away.

When Labels Lead to Anger

"Sticks and stones may break my bones, but words will never hurt me." You probably have heard that old saying before. The truth is that some words *do* hurt, which can make you want to lash out in anger and hurt those who have hurt you.

Sometimes, attempts at revenge may take the form of vicious rumors or pranks. Other times, revenge may lead to violence. The most gruesome effects of labeling and social pressures that our generation has seen have been school shootings. Violence as a result of social pressures isn't a new phenomenon, but the recent wave has brought even more attention to the harm that labels and peer pressure may cause. Violence never solves anything. In fact, it leads to even more problems.

As you probably know, anger can make you feel out of control. You may actually lose control and turn to violence, hitting people or knocking them down. Even worse, you may consider bringing a weapon to school to threaten someone who has hurt you or angered you. You can't solve a problem with a weapon. You may think about hurting someone, but you're in the danger zone if you actually begin to plan out what you're going to do.

Talk to an adult or contact the APA resource in the "Try It!" box on page 73 if you're considering a violent act to get back at people who have angered you. I recommend that you go to someone older, instead of turning to a friend your age for a problem like this. An adult will know better what to do to help you. You can talk to a parent, a relative, or an adult at your school or place of worship.

Stop and think for a moment. Does it make sense to forever alter your life or the lives of others through a violent act? High school is a small part of your life, lasting only a few years (though it may seem like more). It's important to find ways to express your feelings of anger, hurt, and frustration.

Keeping yourself safe is important, too. Don't let the way that someone else sees you make you feel as if there's nothing to live for anymore. There is life after high school! If you're so angry and hurt that you're considering suicide, find a trusted adult you can talk to right this minute. Don't wait. You're worth so much more than any label that people may give you. Never forget that.

TRY IT!

If you're online, you can find sites that may help you with anger or suicidal feelings:

According to the American Psychological Association (APA), you can manage anger through relaxation, problem solving, and better communication. For more information on anger management from the APA, try its Web site *www.apa.org*. Search under "anger" or go directly to the anger-management page at *www.apa.org/pubinfo/anger.html.*

Suicide Awareness Voices of Education *(www.save.org)* promotes awareness about suicide and clears up misconceptions about its causes. At the site, you'll find many articles on how to get help for yourself or a loved one.

There are lots more resources like these on pages 133–136.

Remember that, in the end, labels are just words. Words are lifeless, until someone says one aloud and gives it a voice and a meaning. You give a label power only if you use it to try to hurt someone—or if you let the label define you. If you're a label-user, see Chapter 7, "How to Help Yourself," on pages 120–123 for ideas on how to stop. If you're the one being labeled, I think the best defense is to crush the label before you become affected by it.

Believe in yourself and be confident about who you are and what you can give to the world. (Chapter 7 will give you tips on this, too.)

I'll leave you with some simple advice that a friend once gave me; it still helps me feel better on days when everything that could go wrong does go wrong. "If you have a bad day, the next day *will* be better." In other words, at least you've got *something* to look forward to.

Maybe tomorrow won't be the day you start feeling confident or when people will finally stop labeling you. It may take time for things to improve—maybe a few weeks or months from now, or perhaps even after you graduate from high school. The point is that your high school isn't the whole world. We're young. The world is out there for us, and there's no reason to think that our lives won't be spectacular just because high school sometimes can be rough. Hang in there!

> "They're just labels. What's on the label is not what's in the package."
> —Girl, 16

When Asked...

Do you think girls are labeled more often than guys, or vice versa? Or do you think that labels affect girls and guys equally?

Teens Answered...

(Girls are labeled more often)

"Actually, I kind of think girls are labeled more. I mean, there are a hundred names just for girls (slut, whore, bitch, etc.), but none *just* for boys."—*Girl, 13*

"Girls are labeled more. A girl can do something that a boy does all the time—she gets called names, but he's 'the man.'"—*Guy, 16*

"Girls do, because if we have sex with a guy it is a big mistake for us, but the guy is some big hero."—*Girl, 15*

"I think girls are labeled more than guys, because usually when someone else is labeled it is usually done by a girl or a group of girls, because they feel it's necessary to make themselves feel better about the way they look, act, or dress."—*Girl, 15*

"Girls are usually labeled more than guys, but that is usually because girls do most of the labeling, and there is a need to categorize other girls."—*Girl, 15*

"Girls are labeled more often than guys. Guys are just 'jocks' or 'geeks,' but there seems to be many types of girls, like sluts, goody-goodies, jocks, nerds, quiet people, etc."—*Girl, 16*

☐ "I think that girls are labeled more because girls do more labeling in general. And when guys do label, it's about a girl."—*Girl, 16*

☐ "Girls are more easily labeled as sluts, but I know guys who are sluts—they're labeled as heroes because they've 'had' so many 'chicks.'"—*Girl, 16*

☐ "I think girls are labeled more because there are a lot more names that girls get called than guys, and I think it's the guys that make up those labels."—*Girl, 15*

☐ "I think that girls get hit the hardest with labels because we make ourselves targets for labels. I am not too sure why. We just do."—*Girl, 16*

☐ "I think girls are labeled more often, because they are judged more on their appearance than males."—*Girl, 16*

☐ "I think girls are labeled more often than guys because girls usually do the labeling."—*Girl, 16*

☐ "Girls are labeled more than guys because girls are more judgmental of each other, and they get jealous easily."—*Girl, 16*

☐ "Definitely, girls get labeled more than guys; girls are very competitive."—*Girl, 17*

☐ "I think girls tend to get labeled more because girls are quick to judge anyone who makes them feel inferior, whereas guys just don't care."—*Girl, 17*

☐ "I think they affect girls more often because girls depend on social status."—*Girl, 15*

☐ "Girls are affected more, because no matter how we try to deny it, we are more self-conscious."—*Girl, 13*

☐ "I think girls are labeled more since we fight for the top spot, and we always judge each other on looks."—*Girl, 16*

"I think it affects girls more because girls are known to be the goody-goodies and more responsible. When a guy messes up, it's easily forgiven or forgotten, unlike girls . . . their reputation is hard to keep and fix."—*Girl, 15*

"Girls are labeled more extremely as far as sexuality is concerned. You haven't heard of many male sluts."—*Guy, 16*

"Girls more often than guys, especially on sexual standards."—*Guy, 16*

"Yeah, because girls, have the reputation of being 'perfect' so if they do one thing wrong, it goes around the school and they get labeled."—*Guy, 15*

"Girls. Because if a girl does anything, there is a label. But for a guy, he's just 'chillin.'"—*Guy, 15*

"Girls are labeled more because girls are more easy to mess with."—*Guy, 16*

(Guys are labeled more often)

"I think that guys are labeled more than girls. You hear a lot of names that girls would not be called."—*Guy, 14*

"Guys are labeled more because we are more competitive, but I think that labels affect girls more."—*Guy, 15*

"Guys are more often labeled, because people are less sensitive around guys, but girls are called 'slut' more than guys."—*Guy, 15*

"Girls probably are labeled less than guys."—*Guy, 16*

"I think guys are labeled more often than girls because guys are a little meaner with other guys. I think girls are more kind to one another."—*Guy, 13*

"Guys, they have more stereotypes."—*Girl, 15*

"Guys are labeled more because they usually show off more."—*Guy, 16*

"Guys call each other things to pick on one another. Nothing is really meant by saying these things."—*Girl, 16*

(Girls and guys are labeled equally)

"Girls get a lot of labels, but so do guys. If a guy sleeps around, he's a 'pimp.' If a girl sleeps around, she's a slut. What a world."—*Girl, 15*

"I think it is balanced because girls can be called 'hoes' and guys get called players, and both get called by the group they hang out with."—*Girl, 15*

"Really equally; mostly they're labeled by their friends of the same sex."—*Girl, 15*

"Equally. It all usually depends on race, skin color, any other body differences, backgrounds, who they hang out with, or how they behave or act."—*Guy, 14*

"We guys are labeled as much as girls, but girls may deal with it better."—*Guy, 14*

"I think that they are both labeled equally, but I think that the labels on girls/women are much more harsh." —*Guy, 17*

"Equally. It is just sexist dribble to say that one sex gets labeled more than the other."—*Guy, 17*

"Equally, because I think everyone is labeled at least once in their life."—*Guy, 17*

"I think it is about equal in terms of numbers, but girls receive more insulting, judgmental labels."—*Guy, 15*

"It's equal. But girls get the short end of the stick, because they have labels like slut and 'ho.'"—*Guy, 15*

"I think it's a combination of both. For example, girls are called sluts if they have sex with people, but for guys it's a good thing to have sex—they get applauded for it. I also don't think boys care what they're called as much as girls do, because girls are more sensitive about those things."—*Girl, 17*

"I think that both genders are labeled equally, because both males and females put down less populars with not-so-nice labels and elevate their friends in the completely opposite way."—*Guy, 15*

"Who cares? Everyone gets a label—both boys and girls. Not to be hostile, but labels are a necessary evil."—*Girl, 15*

"Equally—we both get our share of labels."—*Girl, 16*

"It's equal, but girls are more likely to be the labeler and they're more likely to be cruel about it. Guys label and then don't change their minds."—*Girl, 16*

"Equally but girls get different labels than guys mainly because the two sexes do different things. Not to be a sexist, but boys are more jocks than nerds. And girls are more drama queens than techies."—*Girl, 15*

"I think it's pretty much equal. I mean I think there are more labels for girls, but guys are labeled just as much. Just not in such variety."—*Girl, 15*

"I think it's pretty equal. Some labels fit any gender, and girls have as many labels for guys as guys do for girls." —*Girl, 16*

"Equally, because no matter who you are or where you're from, you will always be labeled."—*Girl, 14*

CHAPTER 5

Guy vs. Girl Labeling

"Labels affect both sexes: they both have feelings . . . most guys just hide it—but they hurt, too."
From the Teen Labels Survey

The Teen Labels Survey had a question about whether girls or guys are labeled more often, or if they're labeled equally. Turns out, the teens who responded to the surveys had strong opinions about this topic! (See pages 75–79 for highlights of their responses.) Have you ever thought about the ways in which girls and guys are labeled? Are some labels specific to guys—and others to girls? Or do labels generally apply to either sex? There are no easy answers to these questions.

So, who's labeled more often? Girls said girls were. Guys said girls were. Girls said guys were. Guys said guys were. And some survey respondents agreed that *everyone* has it equally bad. Not exactly a consensus.

Who's doing all this labeling, anyway? According to the surveys . . .

Girls label girls:

"Girls all rip on each other whenever they get mad."

"Girls are labeled more often than guys because girls have a lot more jealousy and hatred toward each other and are always trying to feel like they are above other girls."

"Girls are labeled with more offensive terms. In our school, though, it is the women that label the other women."

Guys label girls:

> *"Girls are labeled by guys faster."*

> *"Girls are labeled more because they can be labeled sluts and other bad things by guys."*

> *"Guys are usually the ones that do the labeling—whether they think the girls are sluts, goody-goodies, or dorks, they are always calling girls by some name."*

Guys label guys:

> *"Because a guy must have power over other guys."*

> *"Guys are labeled more by their guy friends who are mean to them or make fun of them more often."*

Girls label guys:

> *"I think girls label other people more often because it's gossip."*

> *"At our school, guys are usually labeled as jock, punk, goth, or thug and girls are usually just thought of as popular or not popular."*

Does this help clear up the confusion for you? It didn't for me, either!

Girls and Their Labels

I think girls get a really bad deal when it comes to labeling. (Guys get a bad deal, too, but girls even more so.) After looking at the surveys, I realized that girls often are given labels with negative sexual connotations. Think about labels like skank and slut, which are mostly for girls. Girls who are called these labels are usually looked down on or assumed to be something they're not.

> "Girls are labeled more as sluts and whores, regardless of their sexual habits."—Girl, 17

Guys don't get these kinds of labels. Even if a guy is called a slut, a player, or a pimp, he's not necessarily looked down on. He may be admired or praised for his way with girls. The assumption is that his behavior is just fine in the eyes of society.

According to the surveys, girls get more labels—and nastier ones. Have you ever heard of a guy being called a cheerleader, ditz, teen queen, or teenybopper? Probably not. These kinds of labels are mostly reserved for girls. Although these labels don't have a sexual meaning, they *do* have negative connotations. The stereotypes they suggest are that girls are (1) dumb, (2) flaky, or (3) only interested in shallow, girly, unimportant things.

> "Girls get bashed a lot harder if they get around even a little bit—'slut, skank, ho, trashy, dirty,' etc."—Guy, 16

Many girls who responded to the Teen Labels Survey felt that they were judged too harshly. Think about the five factors from Chapter 2 (see pages 27–46):

1. Clothing Style/Appearance
2. Interests/Activities/Music Preferences
3. Behavior/Personality
4. Grades/Intellect
5. Friends

When it comes to girls and guys, these five factors apply a bit differently. According to the teens who responded to the surveys, clothes and bodies are key in determining how girls are labeled. A girl in tight, short, or small clothes may be labeled a skank, just because of what she's wearing. (That's a judgment.) A girl who has large breasts may be labeled a slut, whether or not she dresses to play them up.

> "I think that girls are labeled most often because we're expected to be 'pretty and blond' and if we're not, we're labeled as 'ugly' or 'outcasts.'"—Girl, 15

(Another judgment.) A girl who dresses conservatively or doesn't date much may get the prude label. (Judgments again.) A girl who's into fashion, pop music, or cheerleading may be thought of as superficial because of her interests. (That's a judgment, too.)

> "In my experience it's girls who are more often labeled and more affected by those labels, because as teenagers, girls struggle more with self-esteem issues than boys do."—Girl, 16

Something interesting that came up in the surveys is that labels like goth or punk—which can be for girls or guys—suddenly have sexual connotations when applied to girls. So, goth or punk girls often are assumed to be sluts and are called that as well.

Why is this? Maybe when someone is uncomfortable with a particular group of people, he or she looks for other ways to belittle them or make them feel bad. Calling a girl from that group a slut serves this purpose.

These judgments on girls are part of a double standard that exists today, in a supposed age of equality. What is socially acceptable (or encouraged) behavior for guys is behavior that girls may be condemned for. This is most obvious when it comes to . . . what else? Sex. Boys often are praised for having sex, while girls get called ugly names or are labeled sluts.

It doesn't matter whether the girl has had sex—even if she's a virgin, she could be called a skank or slut. For a girl, simply hanging out with the wrong guy, wearing a short skirt, or having a couple of boyfriends in the same school year can be enough to get these labels. For guys, clothes usually don't wreck or establish sexual reputations.

Is slut a harmful word? A damaging label? Even a slur? (For more about slurs, see Chapter 6, "Slurs and Other Hate Words," on pages 91–107.) Most everyone agrees that it's not a compliment—at least not for girls—but how much damage it can do is open to interpretation. Many people believe that it's just a word, and that it doesn't really mean anything, other than being an obnoxious putdown. For many girls, though, the slut label is a painful reminder of the double standard, and it hurts a lot.

> "Girls are labeled more because people are quick to judge a girl by how she smells, dresses, acts, or looks—but no one ever really says much to a guy."—Girl, 17

Guys and Their Labels

On the Teen Labels Survey, everyone agreed that guys get labeled and they label others. Beyond that, there were doubts about how much guys are affected by their labels. Do they blow off labels or take them personally? How do guys *really* feel about labeling?

According to the surveys, girls tend to think that guys don't care or aren't bothered by their labels. Some guys would agree. Why? The answer may lie in the perception that guys are labeled for different reasons than girls are. Most guys don't feel that their labels have as much to do with their physical appearance or their clothes. Unlike girls, guys aren't judged so harshly about their sexuality, either. Sure, people notice when a guy is attractive, but they probably don't look at his clothes to determine how many people he's slept with. To be fair, there aren't a lot of clothes designed to show off guys' bodies and make them look sexy.

According to ideas in our society, guys aren't supposed to take too much of an interest in how they look. If they do, they run the risk of being called "gay" (read more about this in Chapter 6, "Slurs and Other Hate Words," on pages 97–100) because clothes

> "Definitely, girls are more affected by labels than guys. I think it's because girls are way nit-picky and self-conscious and guys are just like 'whatever.'"—Guy, 17

and concerns about attractiveness are so closely tied to ideas of what's feminine. This is a twist on the double standard I mentioned earlier. In this case, guys who are into their appearance may be criticized for not being masculine enough.

What's more, guys are mostly labeled because of their interests or activities (like skateboarding or music). Is this true at your school? Are guys more often the ones who are labeled as punks, goths, raverz, gangstas, hip-hoppers, hippies, skaters, thugs, gamers, or jocks? Unlike girls, guys usually get labeled based on what they *do* versus how they look. This is a double-edged sword, though. The labels *still* lead to a judgment. The judgment is that guys are troublemakers. Period.

> "The guys I hang out with don't seem to care what people say or think about them. The girls, on the other hand, aren't necessarily more affected by it but they dwell on it. Guys just forget it and move on."—Girl, 16

People might assume that, because you're a male who listens to rap, you're a thug looking for a fight. Or maybe you're into punk music, in which case you may be seen as dangerous and scary. Perhaps you're a skater, and people jump to the conclusion that you have no manners; you may even be banned from skateboarding in public places because you're seen as a nuisance.

I WAS LABELED, TOO...

I would like to clear up my label! I'm a guy who's into inline skating. A lot of older people see me skating and they say, "Oh, look at that little punk," but I'm not. I am just a normal kid. I get okay grades in school, and I like to hang out with friends. There is just the occasional bad

apple who ruins it for everyone. People should think of skating as a sport. It is just like soccer, football, or lacrosse. There is no harm in it. That is all I have to say.
—*Anonymous*

. . . AND I'M MORE THAN A LABEL

Goth guys are most often associated with stereotypes of being dangerous. In the surveys, some guys who were into goth culture said they'd been accused of being Satanic. One survey respondent said he is asked all the time if he is a member of the Trenchcoat Mafia. Remember the media mentions of the Trenchcoat Mafia after the Columbine High shootings?

Under the influence of these stereotypes, people further assume that *groups* of guys are especially threatening. This may be true whether you're part of a gang, a football team, a theater troupe, or a volunteer group.

> "If a woman has sex with a lot of people, she's considered a slut, but guys aren't hated as much when they do that. Labels are equal in a way, though—I've heard guys referred to as druggies a lot more than girls."—Girl, 15

The stereotypes for guys don't stop there. On the Teen Labels Survey, many respondents commented that guys get stuck with drug-related labels more often than girls do. Guys may get called druggies or stoners whether or not they actually use drugs. Teens who responded to the surveys couldn't explain why.

I think the stoner label relates to the stereotype of guys as troublemakers. If you assume that guys in general are looking for trouble and that guys with certain labels (goths, punks, skaters, raverz, hippies) are *really* looking for trouble, it's easy to assume that guys who have those labels are drug users. That's because drugs are more trouble to get into.

> "Guys are thought of as stoners more than girls are."—Guy, 13

How do guys feel when they're thought of as troublemakers and drug users, among other things? If you're a guy, you probably have some thoughts on this. Some guys view their label as a compliment; others simply ignore it. Some are truly bothered by their label and feel that it confines them too much. And others note that even a supposedly positive label such as jock may carry a bunch of negative stereotypes of what it means to be masculine (bully, dumb, overly aggressive, etc.).

Making life more difficult for guys who are labeled is the expectation that they should tough it out and not let their feelings show. Many guys get a cultural message that they can't talk about something that hurts, for fear they may get called *worse* things.

I WAS LABELED, TOO. . .

People have always labeled me a troublemaker. I wear baggy jeans so I must be a thug or druggie. I have bright red hair, so I guess they think I'll hold up a convenience store or something. Because I look different from the accepted idea of normal, people automatically think that I'm bad news—but anyone who actually *knows* me knows that I'm pretty mature and polite. I know I can act like a kid sometimes, but I never do things that I don't think are right. I've accepted the fact that people are going to stare at or criticize me—that's their problem, because no matter what they think, they still don't know the real me. Their loss, not mine. I've also figured out that preconceived notions will always exist wherever you go. I don't let this kind of stuff rule my life, and it *can't* stop me from doing what I'm going to do with my life. So if I want to dye my hair blue or wear baggy jeans and tight shirts, it's *my* decision, nobody else's!—*Anonymous*

. . . AND I'M MORE THAN A LABEL

What Guy/Girl Labels Have in Common

For all of the differences in labels and how they're used on a girl versus a guy, many have become acceptable for both sexes. I call these Equal Opportunity Labels.

These days, labels such as jock, techie, and homie-g are as likely to refer to girls as drama kid, altie, and wannabe are to refer to guys. Even some of the more loaded labels have begun to cross gender lines. For example, some girls have claimed the thug, pimp, and player labels for themselves. Guys may be called sluts, a label they may take a certain pride in. Although the slut label isn't universal yet, it's more common than you might think.

> "Girls have more ability to make bad things good (e.g., 'I'm a bitch!')."—Girl, 15

Some teens figure if you can't beat them, you should join them—or at least *own* the labels and define them on your own terms. By owning and personally defining their labels, some teens feel empowered. They reclaim the power of the label for themselves, put a self-affirming spin on it, and make it harder for other people to use the label against them. They believe that taking ownership of a label in this way helps counteract its stereotypes. You can read more about this in Chapter 6, "Slurs and Other Hate Words," on pages 91–107.

For every person who has reclaimed an ugly label or a nasty name, there are plenty of other people who *haven't* done so. You might want to remember that anytime you're about to use a sexually loaded label. Sometimes, those words may cross the line into sexual harassment or verbal assaults. Maybe you never thought of labels in this way.

Sexual harassment can take many forms, but here are the ones that most closely relate to labeling. Examples can include:

- *persistent or abusive labeling or name-calling* (consistently calling someone a slut or a faggot, for example)

- *spreading sexual rumors* (saying that someone has performed some sort of sexual act with someone else, such as "Did you hear he sleeps with guys?")
- *sexual graffiti* (like the classic, "For a good time call so and so," or scrawling slurs on lockers or bathroom walls)
- *"rating" people* (commenting where someone falls on a one-to-ten scale of attractiveness, "do-ability," or sexual prowess, usually within hearing distance of the person being judged: "I give her an eight—I'd totally do her," etc.)

Whether it's cliques or individuals doing these behaviors, the victims feel miserable. A girl who is harassed may end up thinking less of herself. Eventually, other people may think less of her, too. It's not just boys who harass, either. On the Teen Labels Surveys, respondents said that girls are just as guilty of these behaviors toward other girls.

Maybe you're wondering if guys can be sexually harassed. The answer is yes. Guys can be harassed by girls or by other guys. Any kind of sexually loaded label or commentary could possibly cross the line to unacceptable.

Homophobia is a fear of homosexuality, often shown by extreme dislike, name-calling, or violence.

A common form of harassment is accusing a guy of being gay (possibly using the slur faggot) and labeling him that way. This kind of label can make a guy feel angry or threatened, whether he's gay or not. For guys especially, this type of harassment can be very homophobic in nature. (For more on homophobia, see Chapter 6, "Slurs and Other Hate Words," on pages 97–100.)

How do you know whether a behavior is sexual harassment or not? If someone calls you a whore one time, for example, is that person guilty of harassment? Some schools have a zero-tolerance policy, but more often, a case must be made that the harassment is ongoing or interferes with someone's ability to participate in school life (in class or extracurricular activities) with a feeling of safety and comfort. A one-time incident may feel unsafe or uncomfortable, but it may not qualify under the legal definition of sexual harassment.

If you're a victim of sexual harassment, talk to someone right away. Your school should have a set of procedures you can follow to make a report. The first and most important step is to report the incident to your principal, a teacher, a guidance counselor, a coach, or someone in the administration. It's very helpful to bring a record of the events, or concrete proof if you have it (emails, pictures, notes).

83% of girls and 79% of boys have experienced some form of sexual harassment in school.*

If you believe that sexual harassment is a problem at your school and there isn't a procedure in place to address it, you might consider raising awareness about this issue. Talk to a teacher or your principal. Perhaps a change in policy starts with you.

This chapter is called "Guy vs. Girl Labeling," but I think, in many ways, we're on the same side. We're all *against* stereotypes, aren't we? And if so, aren't we *for* the right to be individuals? We've got even more common ground than that because all of us are affected by labeling in some way. We *all* have feelings about labels—some positive and some negative.

Maybe your label helps you feel good about yourself and your place in the world, or maybe it grinds you down and leaves you feeling as if you're on the outside. Either way, there's so much more to who you are and what you feel. That's true for everyone—guys and girls alike.

*American Association of University Women. *Hostile Hallways: Bullying, Teasing, and Sexual Harassment in School (Survey)*. Washington, DC: AAUW, 2001.

CHAPTER 6

Slurs and Other Hate Words

"I've been labeled based on my ethnic and religious
backgrounds, and my sexual orientation. I've also been
labeled because of certain beliefs I stand for and activities
I'm involved in. Every aspect of my existence has been, at one
point, labeled and insulted—my intelligence, my speech, my
manner, my attitude, my very way of breathing."
From the Teen Labels Survey

You might wonder why I'm including a chapter on slurs in a book
about labels. After all, talking about slurs could take up an entire
book itself. The short answer is, this chapter is here because of you
and other teens like you. On the Teen Labels Survey, many teens
said they'd been labeled because of their race, ethnicity, or heritage;
their religion; their sexuality or sexual preferences; or all of the
above. At first, I was shocked while reading the names these teens
had been called. I was saddened that such derogatory words are a
part of many teens' everyday lives. I didn't want to use these words
in my book. But after thinking about it more, I realized that, if teens
hear hate speech every day, I *have* to write about it.

READERS' ADVISORY LABEL:

There are shocking words in this chapter, which may be offensive
to some readers. My intention isn't to offend anyone.
I want to explain why these words are offensive, how much
they hurt, and what we can do about them.

When I first came up with the idea to write a book about labels, I planned to focus on the social labels that are common today—geek, stoner, teen queen, jock. (Take a look at the Labels List on pages 14–15 for a refresher.) But in the surveys, many teens said that racial, religious, or sexual hate words were their personal labels. To me, these aren't *labels*. I believe that names intended to insult a person's race, religion, or sexuality are slurs.

Slurs are hate words like nigger, dyke, cracker, white trash, chink, gook, flip, JAP, kike, faggot, flamer, queer, bitch, whore, ghetto, towelhead, Jesus freak, gimp, crip, and retard, for a start. This makes for some stomach-churning reading for most people. If the Teen Labels Survey is any guide, teens are exposed to all of these slurs and more all the time.

Slurs attack the core of who you are—the fundamental you. These hate words aren't based on the clothes you wear or the friends you hang out with. The words cut down *who* you are and *how* you are: your immutable identity.

Slurs are worse than labels—much worse. These words hurt more deeply because they show contempt for things you can't change about yourself: the sex you were born, your skin color, your sexual orientation, being in a wheelchair, having dyslexia, your first language, or the religion you've been raised in. It's very painful to have the core of your identity or aspects of your individuality attacked in these ways.

Slurs can be used to target anyone: Individuals and groups. Girls and guys. African Americans, Asians, Latinos, Arabs, Caucasians, Native Americans, Pacific Islanders, and people of mixed race. Gays, lesbians, bisexuals, and transgender teens. People with disabilities. Catholics, Protestants, Jews, Mormons, Muslims, Hindus, and Sikhs. People perceived as being one of the above. Do you see yourself anywhere on this list? I do.

I've had my own experiences with slurs, and one instance really sticks out in my mind. In junior high, I went to a Valentine's dance with a group of friends. I was hanging out at Barry's* table; he was one of the most popular boys in school at the time, and I thought it was pretty cool to be sitting with him. We were having

*Barry isn't his real name.

fun, and I was enjoying myself. Then another boy picked up a candy bar off the floor and was going to eat it. Barry began arguing with him, saying the candy bar wasn't clean. I was surprised. Barry was popular, but he wasn't known for his hygiene (none of the seventh grade boys were).

And then Barry blurted out: "Don't touch that. A nigger could have touched it." I felt my world stop as soon as the word left his mouth. I was stunned and shocked. I had just been laughing and goofing around a few moments earlier. Now the dance was ruined for me. Yet, I said nothing. Where was my sharp rebuttal? To this day, I don't know why Barry said what he said or why I remained silent.

I heard Barry whisper, "She didn't hear me. She didn't hear me." His attempts to cover his actions were pitiful. Everyone knew I had heard him. I whispered to my friend that we should go. We got up, and as soon as we were out of earshot, I began to cry. No one came to my defense; no one apologized.

Maybe you've had your own experiences with hateful words and the weight they carry. Even if the words were used in a supposed joke, and even if the person who used them said, "I didn't mean anything by it," you probably felt hurt, angry, scared, or offended. Who wouldn't?

It's true that slurs are only words, and words don't have power unless you give them power. Still, hate speech generally does what it's intended to do—it makes you feel hated. It takes a very strong person to stand up to that kind of talk. Looking back, I wish I would have stood up for myself at the Valentine's dance, but I was so shocked at the time. Even though Barry hadn't directly called me that slur, I should have told him not to use the word at all.

I often wondered what would have happened if I were Caucasian and had heard Barry's comment. Because it wouldn't have been directed toward me, would I still be hanging out with Barry—even if I felt offended by what he said? What if, that night, Barry had made a derogatory comment about any other ethnic group and I'd overhead that instead? What would I have done? I know I never would have laughed, but would I have stayed friends with Barry and all those other people? Would I have kept quiet, like all the others did, and let him get away with that?

Racism

On the Teen Labels Survey, many teens reported being victims of racial and ethnic slurs. Students of Asian, Native American, African-American, Caucasian, Middle Eastern, Latino, and other heritages all discussed the racial and ethnic slurs they'd heard or been victims of. Teens from different parts of the nation had been singled out in different ways. For example, Hmongs were singled out in Minnesota, Latinos in California, Dominicans in Florida, Inuits in Alaska, and Puerto Ricans in New York. I wasn't surprised to find out that teens had experienced prejudice, but I was surprised at its extent in schools today.

> "One term, 'Gandhi,' was used to portray that I was different from all the American Christian people that went to my school (I'm Indian). Personally, I have no idea why I was called this name. It may have been because I was a different color than the rest and I had a different ethnic and religious background. I hated being called 'Gandhi' because I was left out of many things."—Girl, 17

Some of the slurs that teens mentioned are part of the effort for groups to reclaim slurs that were used to hurt them in the past. (I touched on this in Chapter 5, "Guy vs. Girl Labeling," on page 88.) For example, the "n-word," as many of us know it, is so loaded with a bitter history of longstanding hatred and racism that many people consider it to be the ultimate insult. Is it a word that people should *ever* use lightly? I don't think so.

> "We have lots of Mexicans and they hang out in the back of the class. We call them 'beaners.' It is not very nice, but that's how we label."—Guy, 13

Yet, all you have to do is turn on some rap or hip-hop music to hear the word (some radio stations bleep it out, though). Throughout the surveys, teens reported that they use a version of the word (nigga) among their friends, as in "Wasup my nigga?"

> "When a black person uses nigga/nigger, it's being expressed as a friendly term. But when a white person says it, it's a racial slur."—Guy, 16

Apparently, some people are fine with these terms, but a lot of people aren't. How has a word this harsh been turned into a harmless hallway greeting?

The debate on reclaiming certain slurs has raged in different communities, including the African-American, GLBT (gay, lesbian, bisexual, transgender), and women's communities. Other words that have sparked controversy include queer, dyke, fag, and bitch. There are no signs of agreement in any of these communities, either.

TRY IT!

Think about where *you* stand in the debate about reclaiming slurs and other hateful words.

ONE SIDE SAYS: It's empowering to take back a slur from anyone who would hurt you with it. This side believes that putting a positive spin on a slur is a good thing.

ANOTHER SIDE SAYS: It's all about the context. A slur, even a reclaimed one, still can be offensive if others outside the group use it in friendly or not-so-friendly ways.

AND YET ANOTHER SIDE SAYS: Using slurs in any way is a bad idea, because slurs are hurtful and damaging no matter who uses them. This side sees reclaiming slurs as self-defeating because it undermines not only the individual but also the accomplishments and history of the group.

Who do you agree with and why?

If you're wondering where I stand on the issue, I feel that slurs are harmful no matter who uses them or in what context. I think people end up becoming desensitized to harmful words. The more you hear them, the less shocking and jarring they may

> "Being called chink really offended me."—Girl, 16

become. And it's not fair for those who are offended by the words to be exposed to them in such a casual manner.

This brings me to the topic of using slurs within your own racial or ethnic group. On the Teen Labels Survey, slurs like oreo, coconut, and banana came up. Maybe you've never heard of these, or maybe you're very familiar with them. (It probably depends on what part of the country you're in.) So, what's the deal with the food theme? These kinds of slurs usually are tied to the idea

> "I've been labeled a nigga because it's a black friend thing."—Girl, 15

that a teen is acting "white"—whatever that may mean. These foods are white on the inside and another color on the outside; the teens they refer to are supposedly into stereotypical Caucasian things and trying to deny their African-American, Latino, or Asian-American heritage. This whole idea is ridiculous, and the sooner we stop using these words to describe each other, the better.

I WAS LABELED, TOO...

The oreo name is something that really used to bother me. I don't have any type of tolerance for bigotry. It confuses me that people can be so naive and closed-minded. In my situation, I thought the word was ridiculous because I really couldn't see what the problem was. After a while, I stopped listening to those people. I couldn't take what they were saying. Black or white, I should be able to listen to any type of music. The fact that I listen to rock and pop music doesn't mean I'm denying who I am—the music appealed to me more so than anything else did. I listen to

rap and R&B, too, but the fact that I owned an *NSYNC CD freaked people out. People couldn't understand who I was. The only thing I was guilty of was being me.
—*Bianca H.*

`. . . AND I'M MORE THAN A LABEL`

Homophobia

Prejudice isn't limited to race or ethnicity. Slurs like fag, homo, and dyke are part of the vernacular of most schools. It's common to hear these words in hallways, the cafeteria, locker rooms, even classrooms. Maybe you don't "hear" them at all anymore. Sometimes, words are so commonly used that you may become desensitized to their meaning and intent. Perhaps you barely notice when *you're* using them.

> "The most harmful label I know is being labeled gay when you're not. It spreads and becomes rumor, and then everyone is calling you gay. I think it's worse than a label. Way worse than a label."—Guy, 14

Want to know the most common all-purpose put-down that turned up in the Teen Labels Surveys? "That's so gay." Teens who weren't well liked or approved of were called not only losers, loners, or freaks but also faggots, queers, or homos. Have you heard these derogatory comments being used at your school?

> 97% of public high school students reported regularly hearing homophobic remarks and slurs.*

These remarks aren't always used to mean that someone is actually gay, lesbian, or bisexual. More often, the slurs put down someone or something. And they hurt—a lot. Being called a homo, faggot, or flamer can hurt a guy's self-image and his social standing.

*From the PFLAG (Parents, Families and Friends of Lesbians and Gays) Web site: *www.pflag.org/education/schools.html*

For girls, slurs like dyke or lesbo are used to show dislike; they also may be used if a girl is doing something that's perceived as threatening, such as joining in a male-dominated activity, being independent, or rejecting a date. Queer is an all-purpose insult for guys or girls. Even when used in a joking manner, these terms are put-downs, plain and simple.

According to the PFLAG (Parents, Families and Friends of Lesbians and Gays) Web site, high school students hear anti-gay slurs like these about 25.5 times a day.

> "Kids who act weird or gay are called queers or fags."—Guy, 13

Teens who are gay, lesbian, or bisexual constantly receive such insults. These slurs are more than hurtful—they also can be scary and threatening. Sometimes, the slurs might be a form of sexual harassment, making it difficult or impossible to learn and function at school. (You can read more about sexual harassment in Chapter 5, "Guy vs. Girl Labeling," on pages 88–90.)

I WAS LABELED, TOO...

Gay teens are everywhere. You may not know this because they are hiding from you. Unfortunately, some people in our society have the idea that gay people are backwards, foul, and disgusting mutants. So being labeled gay ends up making gay people feel as though they're different in a very bad way and that they should be "normal." This desire to be normal, combined with the lack of support gay teens tend to receive from their peers, drives many of them deep into the closet. While some schools apparently are accepting and open-minded (some even have gay-straight alliances and clubs), too many are breeding grounds for hate and intolerance.

At times, I am proud of what makes me different. At other times, I must remain silent and hide the truth. I have accepted the fact that I can't always be myself. I have accepted that, depending on the situation or who I'm with, I have to hide behind a façade to avoid being taunted or insulted because of how I was created.

At my high school especially, I feel that I have to hide. While most of my friends are aware that I'm gay, there are many people in my classes who are hateful bigots. It's not fun being called a faggot. Shielding the truth is one way of avoiding that, but hiding is detrimental to a person's self-image and social habits. I didn't even like myself for a long time because of all the anti-gay slurs I had been exposed to, and it took a while to accept that I was "one of those." I think that if my peers had been more tolerant, it wouldn't have been so difficult for me during what was one of the hardest periods of my life.

We have to learn not to judge people by what we have heard or been told. We also need to work on our use of phrases like "That's so gay." It has become a part of the teenage vernacular, and as a result, people don't even realize what they're saying when they utter it.

The word gay has become synonymous with a word describing something stupid or bothersome, or something you don't like. When you say something is gay in a negative sense, you're insulting and hurting a very large group of people. Let's try to incorporate something fresh into our vocabulary and stop the oppression by choosing to say something other than "gay" to represent those negative things.—*Anonymous*

. . . AND I'M MORE THAN A LABEL

When you choose to use homophobic slurs, you hurt people and that makes life harder for everyone. Maybe you tell yourself that you don't know anyone who's homosexual, so you're not really harming anyone you know. But maybe you *do* know people who are homosexual—friends who listen to what you say and decide it's safer to hide who they are from you. *All because of the words you use.* You may think you know who's gay and who's not, but while relying on old stereotypes, you could be contributing to a friend's fear of being honest with you.

TRY IT!

Have you thought about what it's like for teens in your school who are gay, lesbian, bisexual, or transgender? Consider how they may feel. Where do they fit in? How are they treated? Would you feel comfortable as a GLBT teen in your school, or would you be scared? Do you know any GLBT teens? Are you one? Are you out? Do you feel safe? Write about these issues, or talk them over with friends, if you feel comfortable doing so.

Religious Slurs

Slurs generally attack things that are absolutes—things that can't be changed about your identity. The possible exception to this is religion. In theory, you could change your religion, but often your religious identity is closely tied to your cultural and family identity. (It's not like changing a pair of shoes.) The point is, someone's religion isn't something to mock or attack.

> "I hated being called 'AIDS girl' and 'Gandhi.' They insulted me, my religion, and my culture."—Girl, 17

On the Teen Labels Surveys, teens of various religions reported being teased and harassed because of their beliefs. Christians had been called Bible thumpers and Jesus freaks. Teens who practice a religion called Wicca were accused of Satanism by their classmates or called freaks. Muslim teens were given a hard time about Islam, because so many people don't understand this religion or aren't familiar with its peaceful teachings. Girls, in particular, received

> "They think witch = evil, but I know better . . . that's all that matters. My friends understand that Wicca is harmless, so they think it's cool."—Girl, 16

nasty comments for wearing some form of the veil. Jewish teens were referred to as JAPs (Jewish American Princesses), kikes, and dirty Jews.

It's not simply the slurs that hurt but the assumptions that go with them: If you're Jewish, then you must be rich. If you go to a conservative Christian church, then you must be brainwashed. If you practice Wicca, then you're into Satanism. If you're Muslim, then you're a terrorist. And so on. Not only are these ideas hurtful, they are misinformed.

> "People treated me like a freak because I was so into church and was trying to act the right way, and I overdid it (*sometimes*, maybe?). Anyway, I could *feel* the label and I hated it every day when I had to come to school. I had a sick feeling in my stomach."—Girl, 16

The assumptions are no better than the hate words they justify. That's true for all slurs, not just religious ones. Rather than make fun of people because of their religion, maybe you should ask them about it instead. This will lead to better understanding and less hate.

I WAS LABELED, TOO . . .

I have been forever labeled a goody-goody. I can't stand being called that. It's unfair because as soon as people find out that I'm Mormon, they automatically label me a goody-goody. I guess it's not such a bad thing in some ways, but it's extremely irritating. It's not *what* I'm being labeled that bothers me—but more of the fact that I'm *being* labeled at all. I get labeled mainly because I don't swear, drink alcohol, do drugs, drink coffee, watch R-rated movies, or date (until I'm sixteen). I have a lot more rules, I guess, than most other kids my age combined. Since I follow these rules, for the most part, it's an automatic assumption of: "Oh, she must be a goody-goody."

This does and doesn't affect my behavior. I continue to follow the rules, but sometimes when getting teased for being so "good," I almost want to go and do something bad just to prove people wrong. I won't do that, though, because I don't need to go against my values to live up to other people's expectations.—*Anonymous*

. . . AND I'M MORE THAN A LABEL

Disabilities and Other Factors

As teens noted in the surveys, many other factors may lead to slurs and hate speech. Often, these are factors you can't do anything about: physical challenges or disabilities, learning difficulties, your family's financial situation, or where you live, for example. You can't change any of these things—they're as much a part of you as your skin color and whether you're male or female.

People who stand out for obvious reasons—such as for a disability—are often labeled, slurred, or called names (loser, freak, cripple, moron, retard, etc.). Have you ever heard someone say that something is retarded or that someone is acting like a "tard"? This type of language is used every day

> "I'm in a wheelchair, so I'm associated with the words *disability, handicap,* and *physical challenge* a lot."—Girl, 15

to describe something that's considered ridiculous or someone who's acting stupid. When words like this become a part of everyday speech, people become desensitized to them. They stop thinking about where the words began and what they really mean.

Teens with disabilities who responded to the surveys talked about what it's like to stand out yet be completely overlooked. They said that other people thought of them *only* as disabled and nothing more, and then dismissed them instead of considering them as potential friends. Same with many teens in LD (learning disabilities) classes, who were often called stupid, loser, or worse names.

You might also stand out if you're the poor kid in a rich school or the rich kid in a poorer school. People might take one look at you and decide you're not their type. As teens who took the survey pointed out, this may leave you open to teasing and rude names (rich bitch, homeless, trust fund baby, scholarship kid, and so on). Whether you're teased for being rich or poor, it doesn't feel good.

On the Teen Labels Surveys, some teens from small towns or rural areas talked about feeling misunderstood by teens from more populated places, like suburbs and urban areas. For example, teens in a small Inuit village in Alaska wrote that, "Those who don't know any better think we're poor little Eskimos who live off the land. They think we will attack with spears. They think we live in igloos and kiss with our noses. They think we have no education. But watch us go into their neighborhoods, and we'll be the ones thinking *they* are uneducated and in gangs." Do you find yourself making assumptions about teens who live in places different from where you live? Misunderstandings like these are common. And like the stereotypes associated with race, religion, disabilities, and financial status, they lead to problems between people.

What do all of these slurs and prejudices—whether they're based on race, religion, sexuality, or other factors—have in common? It's not who they target. It's not who uses them. It's *why* they're used.

People use slurs because of:

- **Misunderstanding:** When you don't understand someone, you might assume the person is something she's not. As with labeling, you may even form preconceptions that may be light years away from reality. Also, you may use a few experiences you've had with one group to form a general, biased opinion. For example, if you think that all Muslims are terrorists, you may think it's okay to hassle the girl in your geometry class who wears a veil.

- **Fear:** Misunderstanding and fear are linked—it's easy to be scared of what you don't understand. When you fear someone who's different from you, you may want to hurt that person with your words. For example, if you don't know what Wicca is, you might be scared of a girl who practices it and assume she's into black magic. You may decide to make her a target by calling her a Satanist.

- **Disrespect:** Calling someone a slur or using hate speech is a shorthand insult. It's a simple, direct way to show you don't respect someone. But how can you disrespect people you don't even know, based only on their color or background?

- **A need to tear someone down:** It's no coincidence that bullies use slurs to hurt the people they pick on. Slurs are a quick way to tear someone down. Some people feel better about themselves if they can make someone else feel bad.

- **A need for control:** Maybe someone makes you nervous, afraid, or jealous because he's done something you've wanted to do. Sometimes, perceiving someone as a threat might make you feel the need to get back some control. So, you slur the person to prove to him—and yourself—that you're in control.

Have you ever used slurs for any of these reasons? Have you seen other people use them for these reasons?

Teasing, Bullying, and School Violence

School violence has been on my mind since the Columbine High shootings and the other school shootings that followed. I'm sure I'm not the only teen who's been thinking about this issue. A question that gets asked again and again by students, parents, teachers, and the media is, "Where does the violence come from?" The way I see it, school violence may be the final step in a series of actions that spiral out of control. Slurs may play a role here.

You know that slurs hurt. What starts as teasing ("Hey, look at ghetto boy over there") may be part of a larger pattern of disrespect and bullying. If you don't think slurs can be a form of bullying, think again. Slurs can become verbal assaults—and escalate to harassment, cruel jokes, and vandalism. This may open the door to physical assaults and other kinds of bullying.

Sometimes, victims report the problems and get help. Other times, they may change schools. Some may even attempt suicide. Occasionally, victims of teasing, bullying, and harassment resort to violence. The media has reported that, in the past several years, many of the school shooters were bullied and taunted on a regular basis. They went into school with guns to turn the tables or get their revenge. Maybe they couldn't see any other way out.

There is *always* another way out. I hope you hear that loud and clear. Violence doesn't solve anything. It won't make people who use hate words and who bully others stop what they're doing. What will? I think the answer is promoting more tolerance and peace. Does that sound like an impossible task? I hope not.

If you're a victim of hate words or if you witness someone else being victimized, you might feel afraid, angry, hurt, furious, misunderstood, alone, sad, or even vengeful. Instead of keeping quiet and letting the words and feelings cause you pain, here are ten things you can do:

1. Stand up for yourself. If someone uses a slur, calls you a name, teases you, or harasses you, you might say: "It's not okay to say that. I'm not going to listen to you anymore."

2. Confront someone with confidence. If someone calls you a name, ask the person what he means by that or why he talks that way. His response will probably sound stupid to you and everyone else within earshot. Look the person in the eye to show that you're not backing down.

3. Stand up for someone else. If you see someone being slurred, teased, or harassed, stand up to the person who's doing it and tell her to stop. Let her know that you don't agree with her words or actions.

4. Support the victim. Ask the person to walk with you or sit with you at lunch. Talk with him about the incident. If he feels threatened by it, offer to go with him to tell a teacher, the principal, or another adult what happened.

5. Know when to walk away. If someone picks on you and you sense you're in danger of being physically hurt, have the courage to walk away. Immediately walk toward other people or a classroom, so you're less likely to be followed.

6. Talk with your friends to get some perspective. Your friends can let you know it's not just you who's insulted or angered by hurtful words. Friends can also boost your confidence enough to confront someone or report an incident, or even help you do those things.

7. Report the incident. The adults at your school need to know what's going on. Go to a teacher, a guidance counselor, a school administrator, or the principal. Whether you file a formal report or not, these people can help you—and you'll be helping them, too, by informing them about what's really happening in school.

8. Tell your parents or guardians. By talking to them about these incidents, you'll get the benefit of an adult perspective, while warning them about any dangers you're facing at school. If needed, a parent or guardian can step in and talk to the school.

9. Spread the word. Look at the entire culture of your school to see if it supports the use of slurs, and then decide to do something about it. (See Chapter 8, "How to Help Others," for more ideas on promoting tolerance and social change at school and in your community.)

10. Remember that you're not alone. When you're the victim of hate words, you may feel singled out and alone. But you're not. Nearly every teen who took the Teen Labels Survey had been slurred or labeled at some point. Knowing this may give you the strength to believe in yourself.

What if *you* are the person using slurs or teasing others because of their race, sex, religion, or some other factor? Start thinking about why you do this. Is it misunderstanding? Fear? Disrespect? A need to tear other people down or control them? Try asking yourself these questions:

- Which slurs do I use the most? Do I consistently target the same group(s)?
- Do certain groups (and their stereotypes) make me uneasy? If so, why?
- What assumptions am I making when I slur, tease, or bully others?
- Do I feel better about myself after saying these words or hurting other people? Why or why not?
- Is using slurs an old habit that I'd like to break?
- Do I hear words like these at home?
- Do I use hate words because everybody else at school supposedly does?
- What good might come of changing my behavior? What might happen if I don't change it?

To change, you first have to understand why you do what you do. And you have to understand why slurs and other hate words are harmful not only to the people who get called them *but to the people who use them.*

When you use slurs, you close yourself off to interesting people and new experiences. You assume the worst of people you don't know instead of finding out what common ground you may have. You let misunderstandings rule your world. And you open yourself up to hate.

I hope you'll think about the words you use at school and among your friends. You may decide that slurs and other hate words don't have a place in your vocabulary anymore. Language can be a very powerful thing—for bad *and* for good. You can use the power of your words to stand up for what's right.

Part 3
WHAT YOU CAN DO ABOUT LABELING

A MESSAGE TO YOU

Now that you have a better idea of what labels and slurs are and how these words make people feel, you might want to know what you can do to make changes. Maybe you're ready to show people that you're more than a label. Maybe you want to stop labeling others. Perhaps you'd like to get your friends and other people at your school to stop. Are these goals possible? Yes!

In Part 3, you'll learn how to do all of the above and more. Chapter 7 is called "How to Help Yourself," while Chapter 8 is "How to Help Others." I think these titles tell you how to find what you're looking for.

Before you begin, I'll leave you with one short message:

Change starts with you.

How to Help Yourself

"I am who I am. There is no label. There's only a person."
From the Teen Labels Survey

Are you up for a challenge? Here it is: start showing everyone that you're more than a label. Although you can't change people, you *can* influence their perceptions of you. The best way to do this is to be yourself instead of (1) trying to fit a label or (2) accepting how others label you.

Maybe you're asking yourself, why bother? Why try to get people to see me in a new light? I'm not suggesting that you need to give too much weight to other people's opinions. It's not what *they* think that matters most—it's what you think of yourself.

But on some level, everybody wants the freedom to be who they are. It feels great when you can be yourself and be accepted (even admired) for that. It feels good to look around and know you've got friends and peers who think well of you. On the other hand, it hurts when people label or slur you, ignore you, tease you, pick on you, or pressure you.

This chapter isn't about getting more people to like you. It's not about learning to fit in or become more popular, either. There's no way that *everyone* in your school will like you, and as I've mentioned before, popularity is no guarantee of happiness (see Chapter 3, "Labels: A Social Boost?" on pages 50–59). Can you name one person in your life who's unanimously liked and admired? I can't. But you can probably think of people who seem comfortable with who they are. They have the ability to stand up for themselves and stand proud. They don't let the opinions or words of others change who they are. You can be that kind of person, too.

This chapter is about learning how to like yourself, accept yourself, and feel more confident about being the individual you truly are. When you accomplish these goals, people will see you as more than a label. If some of them don't see you as more than a label, your confidence and individuality will still win. You'll be able to tell yourself "Who cares what they think?" with a true sense of self-assurance, and then get on with your life.

Individuality

You might have heard, "He's a real individual," said in a mean, sarcastic way. Often, when someone is described this way, he's labeled a freak. What's wrong with being an individual or standing out? You don't have to be in-your-face unique to be an individual. You can just be yourself.

> "I want to be unique not typical."—Girl, 16

Do you think you don't have what it takes to be a true individual? Some teens consider themselves average or ordinary. And some teens believe that how they look on the outside is the only indication of who they are on the inside. Not true! What's on the outside is the most visible part of a person, but it never tells the whole story.

The truth is, individuality is a characteristic you already have, even if you think you're the most average person in the world. One definition of *individuality* is: "The sum of qualities that characterize and distinguish an individual from all others." Each person is an individual because no two people are exactly the same. We all have traits that distinguish us from other people. That's a *good* thing because the world would be a boring place if we were all the same.

Remember those five factors that influence labeling? (See Chapter 2, "How Labels Develop," on pages 27–46.) Here they are again:

1. Clothing Style/Appearance

2. Interests/Activities/Music Preferences

3. Behavior/Personality

4. Grades/Intellect

5. Friends

As many teens who took the Teen Labels Survey said, these five factors may contribute to how you're labeled. Other factors, such as your race or religion, may also play a role in how you're viewed and treated by others. (You can read more about factors like these in Chapter 6, "Slurs and Other Hate Words," on pages 91–107.)

All of these factors may lead to labels and slurs, but there's *good* news here. They also add up to *who you are*. They're a reflection of your individuality and part of your own unique history. So are

> "Although I may not exactly know who I am, I like to think I know what I want to be."—Girl, 15

your friends. They probably have qualities that you appreciate or admire; most likely, those are qualities you already have or aspire to. That definitely says something about you.

Your individuality is expressed in so many different ways: your clothing, your appearance, your interests and activities, the music you like, your personality, your behavior, your intelligence, and the people you choose as friends. Each of these factors contributes to your identity, just as your race or ethnic heritage does. They all play a role in who you are and someday will become.

Because these factors work together to make you a unique person, you already *are* more than a label. You already *are* more than a stereotype. You are *you*.

TRY IT!

What makes you unique? Get a piece of paper and answer these questions to think more about what makes you the person you are.

Your full name is:
The meaning/significance of your name is:
You've always wanted to:

Your dream for the future is to:
Your favorite time-waster is:
Your favorite movie is (and why):
Your favorite book is (and why):
Your favorite thing to do is:
Songs that could be included in the soundtrack of your life include:
At school, you're involved in:
At home, you always:
In ten years, you see yourself as:
The accomplishment you're most proud of is:
Something you like or love about yourself is:

Hold onto your list of answers. Every so often, look at it to remind yourself of what makes you unique.

Sometimes, living with a label can lead you to lose track of who you are. It's easy to fall into a routine of doing what's expected of you because of your label. You may stop expressing the real you because you forget who the real you is, or because you're scared to be yourself.

One way to start breaking these habits is to find something you like to do. Start with the questions you answered in the "Try It!" exercise on pages 112–113. Is there a hobby or an activity you're interested in but either gave up on or never got around to trying? Now may be the time to pursue it, even if the activity doesn't fit what other people may expect of you. For example, suppose you've been labeled a jock and people think you're not too smart and are only into sports—but the truth is, you want to try out for the debate team. What's stopping you? Do it. Take the risk. Respect yourself and your interests enough to give something new a chance.

As teens, there are so many things we have no choice about. Homework, tests, rehearsals, sports practice, and family time are, for the most part, mandatory. Even if your schedule is already crowded, make time to do things you're most interested in. Start small, devoting at least thirty minutes each week to a new activity. A half hour is only the length of your average sitcom. You can cut out one show a week to make time for yourself.

There's always room in life to make changes. Why wait? Middle school or high school is a great time to find out what interests you and to stretch your boundaries. While proving to yourself that you've got the courage to try new things, you'll be proving to others that you're more than they thought you were. Exploring your individuality and developing your interests will help you become an interesting, well-rounded, and more focused person. Who needs a label when you've got that?

I hope your friends will support you in this. Tell them you're pursuing a new interest and explain why. Don't hide it from them; hiding a part of your life (and yourself) could lead your friends to think you're losing interest in *them*. Your friends may need reassurance that your new interest still leaves room for them. They like being your friends. (Can you blame them?) Most likely, they will be happy for you and will think it's a great idea to express your individuality.

When you believe in your individuality and feel good about expressing it, you're on your way to relying less on any label. And when you're secure in your identity and have an idea of what you want out of life, the labels other people try to give you won't affect you as deeply. This is all part of becoming more comfortable with who you are.

Belief in Yourself

Individuality is only one part of the equation.

Individuality + confidence = the power to believe in yourself.

What is confidence? Where does it come from? You can tell that someone is confident when she walks with her head held high and isn't afraid to look people in the eye. Confidence is an attitude that says you feel good about who you are and what you can do.

When you're confident:

- You treat yourself with respect, first and foremost.
- You have a sense of pride and self-worth.
- You recognize your positive traits and work to change the negative aspects of your life.

- You believe in your ability to develop leadership skills.
- You feel comfortable in your body.
- You make a serious attempt not to compare yourself with other teens.
- You set realistic goals for yourself and try your best to achieve them.
- You recognize that you are more than a label.

Confidence isn't something you're born with or without—you can learn it. However, confidence won't make you a "perfect" person. (There's no such thing as perfection.) Having confidence doesn't mean you'll be 100 percent happy, either. It doesn't even mean you'll always be sure of yourself. So why should you try to achieve confidence if it can't do all of the above? Because confidence can do a whole lot of other stuff for you, including helping you to (1) make friends, (2) deal with life's pressures, and (3) achieve goals that are important to you.

Building your confidence probably sounds like yet another task to add to your already overflowing list of responsibilities. But gaining confidence is critical to believing in yourself. A belief in yourself helps you not to buy into any labels and stereotypes that other people may place on you.

Gaining confidence isn't about repeating reaffirming statements like, "I am the best" or "I am gorgeous and perfect," because confidence isn't a sense that you're all that and a bag of chips. It isn't about feeling superior to others or repeating incredibly ego-boosting phrases to yourself. That's conceit, or a need to brag about your good points, while brushing your weaknesses under the rug. Confidence, on the other hand, involves being comfortable with yourself and accepting your good points—but also being aware that you have to learn and grow.

Here are five ways to build confidence:

1. Learn to handle your feelings. Like every other person, you'll have days when you feel angry, sad, hurt, frustrated, or stressed out. Don't let these feelings overwhelm you. Find ways to let your emotions out—physical activity, talking to someone, writing in a journal. When you learn to cope with your feelings in positive ways, you'll feel stronger inside.

2. Know that you're responsible for your behavior. Other people may try to influence you with their words. They may pressure you to do things you don't want to do. They may put you down to make themselves feel better. Instead of lashing out at these people or letting them talk you into doing something you don't want to do, stop and take a deep breath. Realize that you always have a choice—and that choice is to do what's right for you. Even though it's hard to stand up to pressure or harsh words, you can do it. You'll feel more secure and confident if you do.

3. Become a decision-maker. As teens, we're used to having decisions made by our parents, teachers, or other authority figures. But at this time in our lives, we also get the chance to make more decisions for ourselves: which classes to take, which activities to do, who to hang out with, how to spend our time, and so on. Making decisions takes confidence and *builds* confidence. Give yourself the opportunity to make more decisions in your own life. It helps to ask for advice from friends and adults you trust. You may also want to write down the pros and cons of each decision, and look at your options carefully. If you end up making a choice that you later regret, don't beat yourself up. This is all part of being human. Let yourself learn from your mistakes.

4. Focus on your life—not on other people's lives. It's easy to look around and compare yourself to teens you think are "better" than you. You may see cliques or popular people who seem to have more confidence and power than you do. You may convince yourself that these people are "perfect" and that their lives are so much happier and more interesting than yours. Don't let yourself fall into the trap of comparing yourself to others. Instead, focus on your life and your goals. What can you do to improve your life? Make a list of actions you can take. If you really want to make your life better, start on your list today.

5. Be your own cheering section. Remember all that information about negative self-talk? (See pages 67–69.) Keep in mind that how you *talk* to yourself plays a big part in how you *see* yourself. Tell yourself what you're doing right, instead of focusing on what's going wrong in your life. Instead of "I really screwed that up," you might say, "That didn't go the way I wanted it to, but next time, I'll know the right thing to do."

Most importantly, realize that those difficult moments in your life help you grow as a person. There's a sense of pride that comes from understanding that you can accept the positive aspects of your life, and work to change the negative aspects.

For many teens, it's difficult to develop a sense of individuality or build confidence. We get constant pressure from our peers and from the adults in our lives (parents, relatives, teachers, coaches), and this pressure can lead to a lot of self-doubt. We may spend time questioning ourselves, instead of believing in ourselves. But when you learn to believe in yourself, you'll be better able to handle life's difficulties. Whether you're facing peer pressure, teasing, putdowns, slurs, or labeling, you'll be in a stronger position to stand up for yourself if you realize you're worth standing up for.

To give you an idea of what I mean, I'll tell you a story about a guy named Anthony. He played the guitar well and was the number-one student in his music class. He was kind and generous. He volunteered his time as a music tutor. Some students at Anthony's school labeled him a nerd because he worked so hard in music class. Others called him a rock star wannabe. But he knew he was an excellent musician and a caring person, and he took pride in his accomplishments. When people labeled him or put him down, he reminded himself that the most important opinion was his own. He asked, "How do I see *myself?*" Instead of questioning his talents or thinking "I'll never have a career in music, I'm just kidding myself," Anthony kept working hard. He continued believing in himself.

Belief in yourself doesn't happen overnight. It takes time, effort, and patience. It's worth it, though, because it allows you to be yourself and make the most of who you are.

How to Defeat Gossip and Rumors

> Nothing fuels the fire of labeling like hallway gossip.

People get a false (and fleeting) sense of power when they talk about someone else. It's a "thank goodness it's not me because I'm too good for that" experience. Other times, people get a thrill from putting someone else down or speculating about that person's life.

Spreading gossip and rumors may seem fun, but usually, you're left with a feeling of guilt afterward. If you're the one being talked about, you know it's no fun to be the topic of other people's conversations.

As you work on proving to people that you're more than a label, they may resist the changes you're making in your life. They may bad-mouth you, gossip about you, or spread rumors. What can you do if other people try to undermine your confidence and belief in yourself?

You can:

- **Prove that your label isn't the real you.** Actions speak louder than words, so show people who you really are. Let the real you come through. Suppose you don't want to be called a ditz anymore. You'll need to show people your intelligent, witty self. Raise your hand in class, talk to smart people, and go to the library once in a while. Eventually, other intelligent, witty people will see that you're not a ditz, and word will spread.

- **Confront or ignore them.** People can be stubborn, and if they refuse to forget your label, you have two options: (1) ignore the gossip and refuse to let it bother you, or (2) confront the person who started a rumor about you or is determined to keep labeling you. You might say, "I've heard that you're spreading rumors about me. You know what you're saying isn't true, and so do I. Stop what you're doing. I don't like it." Or say, "I'm more than a label. I don't care what you say."

- **Remind people to consider the source.** Does the person who's spreading rumors or gossip have a past relationship

> "The so-called 'High School Drama' wouldn't be such an issue if people would keep their mouths shut. People could apply more maturity."—Guy, 15

or personality conflict with you? Is it no secret that he or she doesn't like you? If so, then make this known. When other people tell you what's being said about you, you can remind them, "Consider the source." Let people know that the person has an agenda against you and, as a result, the opinion of you can't be counted as truth.

• Get to know people. The only way people can know the real you is if people *know* the real you. Give people a chance to see that you're more than a label and you're above all that nasty gossip. Get out there and meet new people. Join a team or a club. Run for student government. Find some more friends. When you talk to more people, you'll make friends—and friends make great allies. People are less likely to spread rumors about you if they know you and respect you.

TRY IT!

How do you get to know more people? Start by talking to more people. Here are some conversation tips:

1. Project confidence and a positive attitude.

2. Approach people in a friendly way. Smile and make eye contact. Show people that you're interested and you want to know them.

3. Talk to people right before or after class. You might ask them about a homework assignment or suggest going to lunch together.

4. Ask questions. People like to talk about themselves. Find out about their classes, activities, hobbies, or interests. You might say, "I heard you're on the track team. When's your next meet?"

5. If you don't hit it off with someone, don't take it personally or give up. Approach someone else and keep trying.

How to Stop Labeling

How do you stop doing something that may have become as natural as tying your shoes in the morning? Trying to stop labeling might feel strange at first, especially when the people around you are still using labels and slurs. You'll eventually get used to the changes and feel better about yourself, though.

Start by asking *why* and *when* you label. If you discover a pattern in your labeling, you'll be able to stop yourself. For example, do you label:

- when you're with certain friends?
- to impress people?
- as a means of revenge?
- to show dislike?
- because everyone else does?
- because it takes negative attention away from you?

As soon as you understand your pattern, you can be on guard. Next time, you'll probably think twice before you use words like freak, goody-goody, or thug.

Whenever you're tempted to label or prejudge someone, think of D-A-R-T:

Don't use someone's physical appearance as a judge of character. Try to start with a clean slate, even if you've labeled the person before.

Ask yourself questions. How would you feel if you were labeled? How do you feel when people stereotype you? Chances are, you feel bad. Empathy for the other person might prevent you from labeling.

Refuse to let your Label Radar (see pages 61–66) stop you from getting to know a great person. Put your prejudices aside and give people a chance.

Treat this person as you would anyone else you like and respect. Give him an opportunity to show his true character.

You can pay more attention to the way you describe people, too. When you talk with your friends, instead of saying, "Look at the goth over there," try something like, "See the girl with the short blond hair and big black boots? I think her name is Tanya." If you address people by their actual names instead of labels, you'll be sending a message to others that you don't use labels anymore.

Plus, when you identify people by their actual names and qualities, it's clear that you recognize and respect them as individuals. People will begin to gain more respect for you because you're showing respect for others. Your friends might even start to ask you for advice more often. They'll see that you don't let stereotypes influence your opinions of people, and realize how mature and trustworthy you've become.

> "I think all the bad labels should be pulled from everyone's vocabulary because all they do is make people angry. Everyone should be friends no matter how different we are."—Guy, 13

Now and then, a label still may pop into your head. It's human nature to categorize people, but you can resist the impulse to judge them. Keep reminding yourself to be fair and open-minded.

By not labeling, you're taking an active role in your own life. Instead of letting other people's perceptions, misconceptions, and judgments influence your opinions of others, you decide who *you* want to get to know and hang out with. That's a great way to be respectful of yourself and others.

Appreciating Diversity

It's easy to slap a label on someone and not get to know the person. It's harder not to label. But it's definitely possible to stop labeling, and the more you do it, the easier it gets.

To put labels behind you, embrace the variety around you. Live as an example of someone who doesn't buy into stereotypes.

Meet new people at school and in your community. Continue to distance yourself from labels, gossip, and other social pitfalls.

> "I think we should accept anyone—just be their friends. If everyone was accepting and willing, this world would be a better place."—Girl, 13

We are truly fortunate to live in a diverse country. Differences and diversity aren't things to be afraid of, run from, or learn to "deal with." Instead, differences and diversity are something to be grateful for. Living with an open mind and giving yourself the opportunity to meet and interact with all kinds of people will help you grow as a person.

You may find that stopping yourself from labeling and stereotyping has surprising benefits. You'll become a more interesting person because you'll know a variety of people, all of whom can teach you new things about yourself and the world. You'll also leave yourself open to new experiences, different ways of looking at life—and more friendships.

TRY IT!

To meet more diverse people, you might get involved in a summer program that welcomes students from a variety of states and includes diversity as one of its goals. Going to a summer program is a wonderful opportunity, whether you go to an academic summer session, a recreation camp, or a special interest camp for your favorite activity, such as volleyball, dance, or art. You'll meet new people and get a taste for the freedom of life outside of high school. Look for information on summer programs in the guidance counselor's office or school library.

I can almost guarantee that if you make a point of not labeling and you meet a variety of people, you'll find friendship in unexpected places. Friendship is a truly important part of life. Besides our families, we're closest to our friends. In some cases, friends can become a second family. Friendships are so valuable, and true friends can be hard to find. Your true friends are the ones who believe in you, appreciate your individuality, and support you. They help you feel good about yourself—another confidence builder!

One thing to remember: Just because you've decided not to label and you're meeting new people doesn't mean the whole world has had a change of heart. Other people may still label you. Sometimes, it takes a lot of effort to get people to see the real you. Don't give up, though! Keep being an individual. Keep believing in yourself. Spread the message that labels, slurs, and stereotypes aren't okay.

CHAPTER 8

How to Help Others

"School should be more equal and accepting."
From the Teen Labels Survey

By now, you might have taken a good look at yourself and how you use labels. Maybe you've started making the break away from prejudices and stereotypes. What's next? Helping others.

On the Teen Labels Survey, teens were asked what they would most like to change about the social scene at their school. Many teens had interesting ideas about promoting peace in their schools and being more accepting and tolerant of each other. Others expressed how much they would love it if more people would get along more often.

When Asked . . .

If you could change one thing about the social scene at your school, what would it be?

Teens Answered . . .

"That people would take a second glance at others."
—*Girl, 14*

"Include the loners in more things and be more friendly."—*Guy, 15*

"Everyone would know everyone else's name. People wouldn't feel that violence is the only way to be recognized."—*Girl, 17*

"To somehow make people with disabilities more accepted."—*Girl, 13*

"Not exclude people who are different."—*Girl, 15*

"Eliminate boundaries created by a fear of not fitting in."—*Guy, 15*

"I wish school was a total put-down-free zone."—*Girl, 13*

"I wish black people and white people were more together."—*Guy, 16*

"I would make it so people dislike people for *valid* reasons, not because of what they've heard or because of appearances."—*Girl, 16*

"Popularity would depend more on whether you're a good person, and less on how much you entertain and impress people."—*Girl, 16*

"Change the way the popular people treat the not-so-popular people."—*Girl, 14*

"Less gossiping. I would like to meet someone for the first time and not get information about that person through other people."—*Girl, 16*

"We need to work on welcoming the new kids."—*Girl, 15*

"I would eliminate the racist people."—*Guy, 15*

"I'd change the nonchalant attitude towards the use of drugs."—*Girl, 16*

"I would eliminate stereotypes."—*Girl, 16*

"If I had my way, cliques would be gone."—*Guy, 17*

"I'd change the rudeness of some students about appearance and sexual orientation."—*Girl, 16*

"People would stop judging people by what they look like."—*Girl, 15*

"I would want school to be more diverse."—*Guy, 16*

"Everyone would judge people on their minds, not their bodies."—*Girl, 13*

"Everyone would appreciate each other's differences."—*Guy, 16*

"People should respect others a little more."—*Guy, 15*

"I would mature my peers about four years."—*Guy, 17*

"People would reach out and try to befriend one another."—*Girl, 17*

"More overall kindness and courtesy."—*Girl, 16*

"I wish that more people would be themselves."—*Girl, 14*

If you'd like to see changes at your school, the way it can happen is if *you* help make it happen. The social order/rules of your school won't change overnight, but at least you'll be trying to do something positive instead of wondering what high school "utopia" would be like. If you inspire your best friend to join you in making your school a more tolerant place, maybe your other friends will soon follow. More friends may join in, and so might the friends of those friends.

Then, branch out to others: your lab partner, teammates, fellow club members, and classmates. Find teachers who support your ideas for improvements and can help you implement them. Ask these teachers if they notice social divisions and labeling in their classrooms. If they do, they may be willing to help by reassigning seats or rearranging groups once a week for group projects.

You might even consider starting a No Labels Club where students can gather to talk about how labels have affected them and what they've done to deal with bullies, peer pressure, or gossip.

The club could also be a label-free zone where people can feel free to get to know each other and make new friends. Your club might sponsor a Label-Free Day where people are encouraged to meet others, break away from cliques, and stop labeling. You could even make posters that say "Remember Label-Free Day."

I'm not trying to push anyone into going on a crusade. The changes you make can be as big or small as you want. Do as much as you feel comfortable with to start out. You might like the changes you see and decide to do more.

Below is a list of ideas you can get started on. You may want to explore some of these ideas, but not others. You may have a bunch of your own ideas that you want to try. Do whatever you can to promote diversity, tolerance, and acceptance at your school and in your community. Good luck!

25 Things You Can Do, Starting Today

1. Smile or say hello to someone new every day. You'll be surprised at how easy it is and what it might lead to—new friends, for instance.

2. Eat lunch with a different group of people at least once a week. Maybe you eat lunch with the same people day after day. Try eating lunch with people from different classes or activities, or with people you'd simply like to know better.

3. If you find you enjoy lunch with different people, start a Friendly Lunch Club. Model it after the Friendly Supper Club in Montgomery, Alabama, where people gather once a month, and the only rule is to bring someone from a different culture or race for "honest interaction."

4. Expand your social circle. School isn't the only source for friendship. Look for friends in lots of other places: your neighborhood, your community center, a local gym, or your place of worship, for example. Meet people through volunteer activities, an after-school job, or by taking community classes.

5. Don't be afraid to be a leader. A leader is a normal person like you or me, but a leader makes plans, helps organize events and activities, takes action, instigates change, and helps others. You can be a leader, too, by acting on the ideas in this list or coming up with ideas of your own to work on.

6. Start a SHiNE club in your school. SHiNE (Seeking Harmony in Neighborhoods Everyday) is a group by and for teens promoting tolerance and diversity. SHiNE fights discrimination and school violence and helps teens build important skills for success, while getting them more involved in their schools and communities. I've done a lot of work with this group and love their message and their methods.

TRY IT!

Go to the SHiNE Web site at *www.shine.com* to see everything the organization does and offers. It's an exciting place with bulletin boards, essays by students, all kinds of ideas and resources, and information about cool events SHiNE sponsors.

7. Try being a floater. Maybe floater is the anti-label. It's actually a label that means you don't have any label or belong to any clique. Try seeing how many different places you can fit in, while not limiting yourself to one group.

8. Combat cluelessness and cruelty. If you hear someone saying something misinformed or bigoted about another group, call that person on it. Let him or her know that you don't appreciate those comments.

9. Start or run student-led workshops on "obias" and "isms." (As in, homophobia, racism, or sexism.) Invite speakers from local awareness and tolerance organizations.

10. Organize a multicultural event for your school and community. Your event could be a film or music festival, an art show, a polyethnic potluck, or even a talent show. Showcase the cultures of your school's diverse population.

11. Take a stand against slurs. When people use slurs and other forms of hate speech, don't let them get away with it. Make sure they know it's not acceptable language. Talk with your teachers about using class time to raise awareness about these words.

> # TRY IT!
>
> For more information about hate speech, try the Southern Poverty Law Center. The organization uses its Web site *(www.splcenter.org)* and the regularly published *Intelligence Report* to provide information about ways to fight hate. You can also link to *teachingtolerance.org*, which is a great source of information about anti-bias programs and activities being implemented in schools across the country. They publish the semiannual magazine *Teaching Tolerance.*

12. Learn about different faiths by attending a variety of religious services. Visit your local temple, mosque, synagogue, or church, attend a service, and talk to the members of that community. Invite people to attend services at your place of worship.

13. Tackle bullying in your school. Work to get a formal complaint process in place, if there isn't one in your school. Talk to other students about their experiences and see if they have ideas for change. Let teachers know about bullying incidents in your school, instead of keeping quiet.

14. Create a put-down-free zone at school. Make a safe space where students can go—a hall, room, or lunch table. Everyone has to leave their insults and their labels (for themselves and others) behind when they enter the zone.

15. Start (or participate in) a Gay-Straight Student Alliance. Homophobia is all too common in schools, so help fight it. The alliance can combat discrimination with sensitivity training for students and teachers. Give students a safe place to talk about whether they feel threatened in school, are trying to come out, are questioning their sexual identity, or are confronting their own homophobia.

TRY IT!

For information on starting a Gay-Straight Alliance in your school or for other ideas on how to make your school safe for gay, lesbian, bisexual, and transgender students, visit the GLSEN (Gay Lesbian and Straight Education Network) Web site at *www.glsen.org/templates/index.html*. Their mission is to end discrimination based on sexual orientation and gender identity and to make schools safe for all students. The site has a detailed FAQ on how to start a Gay-Straight Student Alliance (GSA), what GSAs are, and how to network with other GSAs.

16. Encourage peer-to-peer mentoring. Start a mentoring club in which older students help support younger ones (and vice versa). For example, sophomores could help freshman get used to life in high school and find their way around. Students who have taken the SATs or other standardized tests could give advice and tips to those who need to take them. Students in any grade could help their peers by offering tutoring services. Peer mentors could also take responsibility for helping to welcome new students who transfer to the school midyear, or who have recently moved to the area and don't yet know many people. All of these efforts will help people in different grades and classes get to know each other better and respect each other more.

17. Raise awareness about people with disabilities. Look at your school through the eyes of someone who has a disability. How wheelchair accessible is it? Are there services for students who may be sight or hearing impaired? What changes need to be made? Talk to your principal about how you can help to make the necessary changes.

18. Learn American Sign Language. It's a whole new way to communicate, and you could even try volunteering your new skills.

19. Tutor other students at your school. You could help ESL (English as a Second Language) students with their English and learn something about their cultures in return. Or you could help tutor students in other grades. Are there ESL interpreters available at school events? If not, you could help make this happen.

20. Take classes in a language that's spoken in your community. Maybe you live in a community with a large Latino population— try taking Spanish. Perhaps there are a lot of Russian immigrants in your neighborhood—take a class in conversational Russian through a community extension course. Check out your local colleges and you might find courses in Hmong, Cantonese, Arabic, or Serbian.

21. Find an issue for activism that cuts across clique and group lines. Choose an issue that affects everyone—the environment or human rights, for example—and get lots of students at your school involved. When working together to raise awareness or solve a problem, it's easier for people to forget about the social boundaries they're used to. Or how about joining together as volunteers for a community effort such as Habitat for Humanity, where you build houses for people in need? Service projects like cleaning up vacant lots, creating community gardens, or volunteering with the elderly are a great way to build unity and promote acceptance. Working together, you can be a force for positive change in your school and your community.

22. Support others in their efforts to change. When your friends or classmates are trying to stop labeling or stand up to a powerful clique, encourage them. Express your support in words and by helping to stop any rumors that may start up. If someone from another group or clique seems interested in getting to know you, be a friend.

23. Be a student/peer mediator. Encourage peer understanding and help people resolve problems before they escalate. If your school doesn't have a program like this, try starting one. Being a peer mediator is a role that lets you become directly involved in issues such as discrimination, bullying, and sexual harassment in your school.

24. Raise awareness about sexual harassment. Do you know what your school's policy and procedures are regarding this issue? If you don't, chances are many other students don't either. Work with a teacher or counselor to get the information out there. Perhaps you could help create a pamphlet that addresses the issue, or organize workshops that use role-plays to demonstrate different forms of sexual harassment and how to handle them.

25. Start a Web site that promotes school unity and tolerance. Create a peer-mediated discussion board where students can address issues and problems in a safe (and anonymous) online setting. Set up a regularly scheduled online essay contest on topics such as diversity, tolerance, and acceptance. Raise awareness about community events and problems as well. You could even start a pen-pal program on the site, giving students in different grades and from different groups a place to connect and correspond.

A Few Last Words

You've reached the end of the book. I hope it helped you think about yourself, your friends, and other teens you know (or don't know) in new ways. You may want to set aside some time to consider how you felt while reading this book and what you feel you've gained from it.

Was there a particular essay or quote that you really identified with? Do you feel differently about a certain label or clique at your school? Are you going to listen more for hate speech and find ways to stop it? Can you speak up if you hear people labeling, using slurs, gossiping, spreading rumors, or bullying others? Will you keep believing in yourself and your power to make changes in your life and in the lives of others?

Your willingness to stand up for your beliefs will help you throughout your high school years—and beyond. You'll become a stronger, more confident, and more open-minded individual. Those are character traits that will serve you well throughout your life.

You are *always* more than a label in my book. Never forget that!

WHERE TO GO FOR FURTHER HELP

Web sites

Bullying.org
www.bullying.org
Devoted to helping and giving a voice to the bullied, this site has hundreds of first-person accounts, drawings, poems, sound files, and films about bullying in all of its forms. It also lists extensive resources and links for all ages.

Gurl.com
www.gurl.com
In the "Dealing With It" section of this Web site is a special feature devoted totally to labels called—you guessed it—"Labels, Labels, Labels." The in-depth history of labels is very informative.

Human Rights Web
www.hrweb.org
An introduction to the Human Rights Movement, this site high-lights current issues, posts relevant legal and political documents, and offers outlets and resources for helping people to get involved with the movement.

Multiculturalpedia
www.netlaputa.ne.jp/~tokyo3/e/
Describing itself as "A Dictionary for Learning Different Cultures the Fun Way," this site picks a question and asks students around the world to answer it. The questions and answers highlight unex-pected differences and similarities between cultures.

Sex, Etc.
www.sxetc.org
This site, sponsored by Rutgers University, is by teens for teens. Teen writers and editors tackle a wide variety of issues including body image, labeling, gossip, gender roles and expectations, love and dating, coming out, stress, violence and abuse, suicide, sexual harassment, and, of course, sex.

Tolerance.org
www.tolerance.org
A comprehensive online resource sponsored by the Southern Poverty Law Center, this site focuses on promoting tolerance through information and action. Its emphasis is on current news, accurate information about hate crimes and hate groups, and concrete ways to deal with hate speech and hate crimes, including "101 Tools for Tolerance" (with tips for schools, communities, and homes) and "10 Ways to Fight Hate."

Books

Flappers 2 Rappers: American Youth Slang by Tom Dalzell (Springfield, MA: Merriam-Webster, 1996). This book discusses the language and labels of youth from the 1850s to the late 1990s in an amusing and accessible manner, offering up surprising tidbits about what's new and what's not.

The Kid's Guide to Service Projects: Over 500 Service Ideas for Young People Who Want to Make a Difference by Barbara A. Lewis (Minneapolis: Free Spirit Publishing, 1995). From simple projects to large-scale commitments, this book offers suggestions for making a difference in politics, the environment, hunger, literacy, and many other areas.

The Kid's Guide to Social Action: How to Solve the Social Problems You Choose—and Turn Creative Thinking into Positive Action by Barbara A. Lewis (Minneapolis: Free Spirit Publishing, 1998). Exciting, empowering, and packed with information, this book offers step-by-step instructions and comprehensive resources for taking practical action on a large number of issues facing teens and the world.

"101 Ways to Combat Prejudice" by The Anti-Defamation League, 2001. Published by the ADL and Barnes & Noble for their Close the Book on Hate campaign, this 32-page pamphlet has suggested readings, a list of definitions, and tips and resources for teens on how to combat prejudice in all areas of their lives. A free printable version (as a PDF) is available online at *www.adl.org/prejudice/default.htm*.

7 Habits of Highly Effective Teens by Sean Covey (New York: Fireside Books, 1998). Sean Covey applies the 7 Habits of Highly Effective People to the busy and stressful lives of teenagers. Whether your goal is to become more confident, make new friends, or just become a pro at time management, this book will help you along the road to success with helpful tips and humorous anecdotes.

Organizations

Habitat for Humanity International
121 Habitat Street
Americus, GA 31709
(229) 924-6935, ext. 2551 or 2552
www.habitat.org
Habitat for Humanity works to provide affordable housing and to eliminate poor housing and homelessness worldwide. Projects often include building or renovating homes for low income families in the various chapter communities.

National Youth Leadership Council
1667 Snelling Avenue North
St. Paul, MN 55108
(651) 631-3672
www.nylc.org
The NYLC's mission is to help young people become leaders in their communities through meaningful service-learning and community involvement.

Parents, Families and Friends of Lesbians and Gays (PFLAG)
1726 M Street NW, Suite 400
Washington, DC 20036
(202) 467-8180
www.pflag.org
PFLAG promotes the health and well-being of gay, lesbian, bisexual, and transgendered persons, and their families and friends. Through support, education, and advocacy, their aim is to create a society that is healthy and respectful of human diversity.

Students Against Destructive Decisions (SADD)
P.O. Box 800
Marlboro, MA 01752
1-877-SADD-INC (1-877-723-3462)
www.saddonline.com
A student-based organization originally founded to combat drunk driving and underage drinking, it has expanded its mission to address issues of risk-taking and poor decision-making such as taking drugs, sex and sexually transmitted infections (STIs), violence, and suicide.

Videos

In the Mix is an award-winning weekly series on PBS that discusses issues facing today's teens, such as labeling, stereotyping, and cliques, in a thoughtful and interesting way. To obtain past programs or for more information or resources, contact: In the Mix, 114 E. 32 Street, Suite 903, New York, NY 10016; 1-800-597-9448; *www.pbs.org/inthemix.*

In the Mix: Cliques—Behind the Labels (30 minutes). This episode addresses the good, the bad, and the ugly of cliques, labeling, and the high school social system as described by the students themselves.

In the Mix: School Violence—Answers from the Inside (30 minutes). This episode talks with teens at a suburban high school. They discuss issues like labeling, the school's social hierarchy, how confrontation between social groups can lead to violence, and what can be done by students to prevent another tragic school violence headline.

In the Mix: What's Normal—Overcoming Obstacles and Stereotypes (30 minutes). In this episode, several teens who live with different challenges that place them outside the "norm" (physical and learning disabilities, deafness, being gay) are profiled. The teens talk about the stereotypes they faced and what "normal" really means.

BIBLIOGRAPHY

Abedon, Emily Perlman. "Crush the Cliques," *CosmoGIRL!* 2:7 (September 2000), 158.

Adler, Jerry. "Beyond Littleton: The Truth About High School," *Newsweek,* 133:19 (May 10, 1999), 56–58.

Allen, Irving L. *Unkind Words: Ethnic Labeling from Redskin to WASP.* New York: Bergin & Garvey, 1990.

American Association of University Women Educational Foundation. *Hostile Hallways: Bullying, Teasing, and Sexual Harassment in School.* Washington, DC: American Association of University Women Educational Foundation, 2001.

Billings, Laura. "Don't Be Bullied!" *CosmoGIRL!* 2:8 (October 2000), 94.

Burby, Liza N. "Clique Power," *New York Newsday* (August 28, 1999), sec. 2B.

Carter, Kelley. "Gay Slurs Abound," *Des Moines Register* (March 7, 1997).

Covey, Sean. *The 7 Habits of Highly Effective Teens: The Ultimate Teenage Success Guide.* New York: Simon & Schuster, 1998.

Dalzell, Tom. *Flappers 2 Rappers: American Youth Slang.* Springfield, MA: Merriam-Webster, 1996.

Dolgoff, Stephanie. "How To Deal with a Bad Reputation," *CosmoGIRL!* 3:7 (September 2001), 116.

Duvall, Lynn. *Respecting Our Differences: A Guide to Getting Along in a Changing World.* Minneapolis: Free Spirit Publishing, 1994.

Forman, Gayle. "Hey, Dork," *Seventeen,* 58:10 (October 1999), 172–176.

Fox, Annie. *Can You Relate? Real-World Advice for Teens on Guys, Girls, Growing Up, and Getting Along.* Minneapolis: Free Spirit Publishing, 2000.

Gaines, Donna. *Teenage Wasteland: Suburbia's Dead End Kids.* New York: Pantheon Books, 1991.

Hatred in the Hallways: Violence and Discrimination Against Lesbian, Gay, Bisexual, and Transgender Students in U.S. Schools. New York: Human Rights Watch, 2001.

Howe, Neil, and William Strauss. *Millennials Rising: The Next Great Generation.* New York: Vintage Books, 2000.

Kaufman, Gershen, Lev Raphael, and Pamela Espeland. *Stick Up for Yourself! Every Kid's Guide to Personal Power and Positive Self-Esteem.* Minneapolis: Free Spirit Publishing, 1999.

Lewis, Barbara A. *What Do You Stand For? A Kid's Guide to Building Character.* Minneapolis: Free Spirit Publishing, 1998.

Massachusetts Governor's Commission on Gay and Lesbian Youth. *Making Schools Safe for Gay and Lesbian Youth: Breaking the Silence in Schools and in Families.* Boston: Massachusetts Governor's Commission on Gay and Lesbian Youth, 1993.

McFarland, Rhoda. *Coping with Stigma.* New York: Rosen Publishing Group, 1989.

Mintz, Phil. "Taking Exceptions," *New York Newsday* (August 29, 1999), sec. 14G.

National Education Association (Human and Civil Rights Division). "Stop Sexual Harassment Now!" Washington, DC: National Education Association (Human and Civil Rights Division), 1997.

Orenstein, Peggy. *Schoolgirls: Young Women, Self-Esteem, and the Confidence Gap.* New York: Anchor Books, 2000.

Peck, Lee A. *Coping with Cliques.* New York: Rosen Publishing Group, 1992.

Romain, Trevor. *Cliques, Phonies, & Other Baloney.* Minneapolis: Free Spirit Publishing, 1998.

Rubenstein, Atoosa. "Hey!" *CosmoGIRL!* 2:5 (June/July 2000), 24.

Scher, Hagar. "Smashing Stereotypes," *JUMP,* 3:8 (August 2000), 86–89.

Schneider, Meg F. *Popularity Has Its Ups and Downs.* Englewood Cliffs, NJ: Julian Messner, 1992.

Sherman, Alexa Joy. "The Anatomy of a Popular Girl," *JUMP,* 4:4 (March 2001), 68–71.

Siegel-Mevorah, Marisa. "Who Are You Calling A . . . ," *CosmoGIRL!* 2:8 (October 2000), middle insert.

Sommers, Michael A. *Chillin': A Guy's Guide to Friendship.* New York: Rosen Central, 1999.

Stern, Jane and Michael. *Sixties People.* New York: Knopf, 1990.

Strauss, Susan, with Pamela Espeland. *Sexual Harassment and Teens: A Program for Positive Change.* Minneapolis: Free Spirit Publishing, 1992.

Tatum, Beverly Daniel. *"Why Are All the Black Kids Sitting Together in the Cafeteria?" and Other Conversation Starters About Race.* New York: Basic Books, 1999.

Trebilcock, Bob. "Dying to Be Popular," *YM,* 47:7 (September 1999), 80.

Waxer, Cindy. "Cliques: The Good, the Bad & the Lonely," *JUMP!* (March 1999), 88.

INDEX

Note: entries in **bold** indicate common labels.

A

Abercrombie, 14, 28
Activism issue, 131
Activities
  and label development, 32–37
  to stop labeling, 113–114, 126–132
ADL (Anti-Defamation League), 134
African Americans, dress of, 30
Alcohol use, 39
Alienation, 69–72
Altie, 14
American Psychological Association
  (APA), 73
American Sign Language (ASL), 130
Amount of clothing worn, 29–30
Anger and labels, 72–74
Anti-Defamation League (ADL), 134
APA (American Psychological Association),
  73
Appearance and label development, 27–31,
  42, 82–83
ASL (American Sign Language), 130
Attendance in class, 38–39
Attitude, superior, in cliques, 46
Automatic labeling, 12–13, 25

B

Band involvement, 36
Behavior, 37–40
Body piercing, 30, 31
Books for help, 134–135
Boys. *See* Guys
Bullying, 104–107, 129,
Bullying.org (Web site), 133

C

Categorization and labels, 25
Cheerleader, 14, 42
Christian slurs, 100
Class attendance, 38–39
Cliques
  as insiders, 53
  In the Mix PBS television series, 136
  and peer pressure, 56–57
  in Teen Labels Survey, 8–9
  vs. friendship, 43–47
Clothing style, 27–31, 42, 82–83

Columbine High School shootings, 1, 86, 104
Computer geek, 33
Computers and technology
  interest in, and label development,
    33–34
  Internet, 20, 132, 133–134
  start peer-mediated Web site, 132
Confidence and helping to stop labeling,
  114–117
Conformity, in cliques, 45
Confrontation
  gossip and rumor, 118–119
  slurs, 105, 129
Consider the source, gossip and rumors,
  118–119
Control and use of slurs, 104
Conversation tips, 119
Coolness and popularity, 54–55
Covey, Sean, 135
Cultural labels, 20–21
Cutting class, 38–39

D

Dalzell, Tom, 134
D-A-R-T mnemonic to stop labeling,
  120–121
Decision-making to stop labeling, 4
Defense of victim from slurs, 105
Demographics in Teen Labels Survey, 7
Diddy, P., 28
Disabilities
  raising awareness, 130
  slurs based on, 102–103
Disco in 1970s, 18
Disrespect and use of slurs, 104
Ditz, 14, 42, 68
Diversity appreciation and helping to stop
  labeling, 121–123
Dork. *See* Nerd
Drama kid, 14, 33
Drama queen, 33
Dress, 27–31, 42, 82–83
Drug use
  and guy labeling, 86–87
  at raves, 39–40

E

Ecstasy (drug), 39, 40
English as a Second Language (ESL),
  130–131

ABOUT THE AUTHOR

Aisha Muharrar attended high school on Long Island, New York, where she was Editor in Chief of the school newspaper for two years, a member of the school orchestra, and involved in many other school activities. Writing has been a passion of hers since she was five years old when she determined that she wanted to create the magic she read in books. She's received numerous writing awards including recognition as one of New York State's Promising Young Writers. She was a member of the 2000–2001 *Teen People* News Team and also served as a volunteer reporter for SHiNE.com (a national nonprofit organization that uses art, music, technology, and sports to engage and empower young people to take a stand, use their voice, and impact their world). She graduated valedictorian of her 2002 high school class and was a recipient of the Harvard Book Award for her scholastic achievements. She wrote *More Than a Label* when she was seventeen years old.

In her spare time, Aisha likes to spend time with her family and friends, listen to music, shop, exercise (dance, yoga, sports), write short stories and poems, and go online. You can usually find her at the bookstore reading stacks of magazines, at home eating fish sticks and watching *The Simpsons,* or driving around in the Blueberry Cupcake.